Strategic Grantseeking for Community-Based Organizations

Strategic Grantseeking for Community-Based Organizations

Using Your
Whole Brain
Whole Heart
and Real Soul

Glenna M. Crooks, PhD

iUniverse, Inc.
Bloomington

Strategic Grantseeking for Community-Based Organizations
Using Your Whole Brain, Whole Heart and Real Soul

iUniverse books may be ordered through booksellers or by contacting:

iUniverse
1663 Liberty Drive
Bloomington, IN 47403
www.iuniverse.com
1-800-Authors (1-800-288-4677)

ISBN: 978-1-4759-8925-0 (sc)
ISBN: 978-1-4759-8926-7 (ebk)

Printed in the United States of America

iUniverse rev. date: 05/28/2013

This book is dedicated to those who come to the tail-end of a program, realize they're almost out of funds, and break out in a cold sweat wondering how they'll keep it going until more money arrives. May these insights help transform them to an easier, more organized, successful and peaceful place I call Strategic Grantseeking.

Contents

How to Access My Workshop Materials

I no longer personally provide grantseeking training and assistance. Nonetheless, I want others to be able to access the materials I developed and used during the time I did.

At www.glennacrooks.com/presentations/grantseeking readers will see a variety of materials, all provided *free of charge* as resources for those who want to use them. These include:

- Workshop Logistics Support,
- Workshop Binders,
- Workshop Powerpoint slides, and
- Grantseeking articles.

The materials contain my brand images—which can be changed if you prefer—and here are examples of how they can be used:

- ***Quote me as an expert.*** Some peoples may need to quote me as an expert. Let's face it, grant proposal writers are not at the top of any organization's food-chain. Whether or not they "know their stuff", far too many grantwriters and their expertise are marginalized. If you're in that situation, like this approach to grantseeking and need to quote an "expert" to get your organization to work in this direction, then by all means, use these slides, my brand images and quote me.
- ***Be efficient.*** Some people will be long on credibility, but short on time. In fact, everyone will be short on time! If you like this approach, feel free to use it—in whole or part—branded as your own organization's process. Pick and choose what works for you; remove my brand images and replace them with yours.

- ***Create or build a business.*** Some people might already be—or want to be—grantseeking consultants or trainers. If these materials help you to create or grow your own business, by all means use them. What a great way to do well by doing good.
- ***Improve member service.*** Some people—especially if they work within national—or state-based membership groups—will have organizational newsletters and may be looking for helpful newsletter or website content. If the articles I provide are helpful as is—or as you choose to edit them—I hope your membership benefits and these make your life easier.

Acknowledgments

Though my experience in grantseeking spans the fields of education and health care, I believe that this proven approach to developing successful proposals is applicable to community development, child advocacy, care for seniors, the arts, environmental protection and other arenas where community-based organizations serve the needs of others.

This book would not have been possible without the guidance and feedback of community-based organizations and individuals in the health and human services arena. It was the dedication and perseverance with which they faced the everyday challenges of serving their communities that inspired me to do this work. HIV/AIDS service organizations, churches and clergy, people using personal funds to help others in need shared experiences and influenced the content you'll read here. The examples I have chosen reflect those communities and the work with them. They faced some of the greatest challenges anyone can imagine as they managed serious diseases while enduring disparities, stigma and lack of funding.

With many thanks as well to all the individuals who helped this project along the way: Laudy Robinson, Curtisy Briggs, Robin Warshaw, Deborah Thornton, Faith Corman and Nancy Zatzman. And finally, to that visionary guy at GlaxoSmithKline who got me started on this and who still wishes to remain anonymous, a special "shout out" of thanks to you again!

Preface

How I Got Here

In my career, I have developed programs, written grant proposals, lobbied for government appropriations, sat on foundation boards, and reviewed foundation and government grant applications. I even created my own foundation with proceeds from another book.

When I was grantwriting, the people I cared about were desperate, and those needs seemed far greater than we could ever address in the small communities or small organizations attempting to meet them. I'd never been trained in grantseeking, was intimidated by the process and always afraid we'd fail.

Yet, we achieved success. Since then I've come to understand the challenges from all sides of the table. I knew the needs of communities first hand, grappled with proposal writing challenges, felt the satisfaction of winning funds and experienced the gratitude at being able to help fund others with some of my own earnings.

I also felt frustration.

Some people may not agree with me, but I've always seen vast resources available for strong programs, even in tough economic times. Regardless, even in good times I've seen good programs go unfunded. I also witnessed tension and frustration between grantors and grantees and between grantwriters and their organizations. Far too often, I saw an unfortunate "scarcity mentality" plaguing virtually everyone in the grantseeking arena. I know from experience that money is not the scarce resource. When a compelling case is made, the money shows up! So, what was going on? Why were good organizations serving their communities failing to secure funds?

I was pondering these questions when an executive of GlaxoSmithKline phoned. He wanted to know if I could help groups improve their proposal-writing abilities. I'd never taught others how to write grant proposals, but reasoned that my own prior experience could be translated into workshops that would help. I was game; so were a small group of organizations who agreed to be the first students. I helped them develop program ideas and write winning proposals. Yes, winning proposals. Right from the start, the approach could be outlined into simple steps that would create success.

As they succeeded, I wondered what we might be doing that was different. I piled my desk high with grantseeking guides to see what they advised. "Hacking in" to my process and everyone else's, I saw patterns.

The first pattern was that most books described *only* the technical "nuts and bolts" of proposal writing. They lacked a personal perspective and soul. Yes, the existing literature on grantseeking was helpful *but* it was incomplete. It lacked important information about bringing personal character, integrity and honesty to the table and neglected the essentials of developing and maintaining high-quality relationships.

This seemed a crucial oversight. Throughout my experience developing programs, writing proposals and reviewing grant submissions, I found that character and connections were critical to securing sustainable funding. Like most things in life, grantseeking is not *only* about budgets, statistics, numbers, programs and business letters. It is about your heart and whether it can connect with prospective funders. It is *also* about their hearts. What you do in grantseeking will help them connect to you, your organization, and your vision—or not. If you are seeking support for your projects, your likely funders are interested in your programs, your budget and your ability to write a clear, proper business letter, but they are also interested in you! And they want you to be interested in them! Grantseeking is not sustainable without connection and reciprocity.

I noticed another pattern as well. All of the groups I worked with had great ideas and most (even the smaller groups) had talented people who were good proposal writers under the right conditions. Unfortunately, most were running in so many different directions that they did not have the time to develop their ideas fully, to craft proposals or to manage the grantseeking process proactively. Proposal writers were isolated within their organizations. They were stressed out and their efforts were haphazard and reactive. The result was last-minute, poorly-crafted proposals that did not reflect the organizations' quality programs, dedication and talented staff. They needed help formulating time-efficient, comprehensive strategies.

In this book, I offer the nuts, bolts and details, *and* ways to help organize the nuts, bolts, details and people surrounding them, in a step-by-step, comprehensive, "big-picture" strategy aimed at creating lasting impressions and lasting relationships.

And the good news doesn't stop there. Groups that used this approach found that not only did they secure more funds, but their organizations transformed as well. This whole-brain, whole-heart, whole-picture and real-soul approach did more than raise money. Instead of being a difficult, tiresome and negative chore, the process of grantseeking infused their organization with energy, vision, focus and collaboration. They partnered with others more often. They discovered assets and allies they'd been ignoring. They got more non-financial help to build their service mission. What could be better?

I believe this approach can do the same for your organization even if—in fact, *especially* if—it's a small one. Just because you're small does not mean you're not mighty!

I hope this can help unify, strengthen and, yes, transform your group—from a hat-in-hand, scattershot supplicant into a well-defined, financially-sound entity that's admired for its integrity, effective services and business skills. I hope this helps you build more robust, better-planned programs, draw on collaborative input at all levels, foster stronger community connections and alliances, support your organization's future, and last, but not least, nourish the whole-heart dedication that the people in your organization and your funders bring to work.

You may be thinking, "I don't have the time or the staff for this!"

It may seem that way at first. But when your organization takes a strategic approach to grantseeking, everyone's time is spent more effectively, everyone's energy becomes more focused, your Board can be more helpful, and your organization's future is more secure.

And the whole process can even be creative and fun.

I'll show you how to do it.

So, let's get going!

Introduction

Successful grantseeking is strategic. It demands attention to product, process and people. Yet too often, not-for-profit organizations forget their primary purpose, are overwhelmed by application details, fail to plan and ignore that their efforts need to sustain long-term horizons. As a result, their grant proposals are inadequate and either denied outright or woefully underfunded.

Whether your group is small or large, it has the capabilities to create successful, winning proposals. What's more, instead of being a difficult, painful and negative experience, grantseeking can infuse your organization with energy, vision, and focus—and secure the funding you need to support and build your service mission.

To achieve that, I recommend a **whole-brain, whole-heart, real-soul approach to grantseeking**. This approach meshes objective and analytical (left-brain) elements with those that are holistic and synthesized (right-brain). It draws on the passion that the heart provides for the work you do and for many people, touches deeply into the soul-spurred dedication for your life's mission. What you get is much more than the sum of the parts. You get great ideas, fantastic teamwork, winning proposals and stronger organizations!

Your group will be **unified, strengthened and, yes, transformed**—from a hat-in-hand, scattershot supplicant into a well-defined, financially sound entity that's admired for its effective services and business skill.

Your clients will get the benefit of your careful planning in better programs, and your funders will get the satisfaction of knowing that they are supporting quality efforts to improve the community you—and they—care about.

Whole-brain, whole-heart, real-soul grantseeking:

- Aligns personal and organizational missions
- Builds healthier, better planned programs
- Draws on collaborative input from everyone, at all levels, involved in the project
- Fosters stronger community connections
- Supports the organization's future
- Promotes beneficial alliances with other organizations
- Nourishes the dedication you and your staff bring to your work.

Right now, you may be thinking, "I don't have the time or staff for this!"

Well, it may seem that way at first. But when you take an integrated approach to grantseeking, your time is spent **more effectively**, your staff becomes **more involved** in program outcomes, your board of directors grows **more helpful** and your income stream is **more secure**.

You'll learn the important groundwork of grantseeking, how to develop a proposal, where to go for what you need, how to nurture funders, ways to achieve funding success, and much more. I've also included select samples of key proposal elements to help you during the planning and writing phases of the grantseeking process.

Chapter 1

Guiding Principles: Honesty, Clarity, and Relationships

"My organization needs money. I'm pushing proposals out the door to every funder I can find, yet few of my proposals are approved. I just can't understand why money isn't coming in to support our important work. I'm losing sleep over how we're going to keep our programs running."

—Community Project Manager

If this sounds familiar, stop for a moment and take a deep breath.

Your next step isn't to make a call, search funding websites, or even to rewrite your organization's previous proposals. It's to pause and think about the three guiding principles of grantseeking: Honesty, Clarity, and Relationships.

Notice, I did not say these are "ideals," they're "principles." Ideals are too often negotiated away as "unattainable," set aside in a crisis or compromised when the going gets tough. Guiding principles, on the other hand, are rock-solid watchwords you *must* abide by throughout project development, proposal writing, and beyond. Failure to do so may doom even your best efforts and hardest work. It has for many others!

Take a "gut check"—a quick, internal evaluation—about how you apply each of these principles to grantseeking currently. If, like many groups, you plunge headfirst into grant*writing*, pursuing funds as an urgent item on your already overly long "must-do" list, it's likely you haven't had the time to consider how these three principles affect your goal. Now is the time to *make the time* to review these guiding principles, apply them to your grantseeking work, and revisit them at every step to help you stay on track.

Guiding Principle #1: Honesty

Your philosophy, message, and actions must be truthful, regardless of who's watching or listening: other staff, funding prospects, clients, or community leaders—in fact, even your friends and family. In this networked world, you never know who the next funder will be or who will influence them to support your projects.

Being honest will demonstrate that you are **worthy of the funder's trust**. Too many funders have seen their resources spent in unintended ways or wasted by poorly managed organizations. Too many good program ideas have been undermined by unskilled remarks about an organization's clients made by project staff at social gatherings. Too much funding has been pulled because site reviewers saw staff behaving in ways that contradicted the stated philosophy of the organization. If you can earn the funder's trust by showing exemplary integrity, you will win much more than short-term gains in funding. You will inspire strong, broad-based confidence in the organization, its mission, and its management. Later, if one program should falter or one individual fails to perform—as sometimes happens—these shortcomings are less likely to jeopardize the funder's support for—and belief in—your efforts.

That means you must practice what we call **"truth-in-asking."** When seeking funds, ask for what your program truly needs. Don't inflate the amount beyond what you actually require or can manage effectively. On the other hand, don't ask for too little, fearing the funder will be intimidated by large requests. Under-requesting is just as dishonest as over-requesting. Think about what you can accomplish, request only that amount and even then, only if your organization can suitably handle such a sum.

It is also essential to be honest about how well your program fits the grantmaker's mission. Don't revise your concept to fit the description in the Request for Proposal (RFP) or the mission you find on the grantmaker's website. That approach too often results in ineffective programs, earns you a reputation as a manipulative grantee, and is counterproductive to achieving long-term, sustainable funding. Successful grantseeking, whether short-term or long-term, relies upon a proven track record of delivering the program results you promised.

This much honesty might seem risky, but it's not. Whole brains, whole hearts and real souls like honesty and function better in that climate. We urge grantees to start with it, and stay with it. When you're desperate for funds, it may be tempting to cut corners and rationalize taking liberties with the truth. The reality is, that's a recipe for disaster within yourself, within your organization, in your programs and with your funders. When you are facing a hard question or are uncertain about which approach to take, take the honesty test first.

Guiding Principle #2: Clarity

Be clear, complete, and organized in your planning and writing. Use direct, declarative statements. Think "concise." Padding looks like what it is—an attempt to enhance a small idea by surrounding it with the "weight" of clutter and lots of type. Funders want solid programs with real results, not the products of magicians who distract them with dazzling tricks.

Avoid buzzwords and jargon. Don't litter the proposal with acronyms or affected words to prove expertise or professionalism. These obscure meaning and work against your effort because they make the proposal harder to understand.

To communicate effectively, **your thinking must be clear before your language can be.** Understand your program idea, staff capabilities, and organizational needs before you set out to request funds. If you are uncertain about any of these critical elements, examine and define them better before going forward.

3

If you have any questions about the clarity of your proposal, ask someone else to review it—preferably someone outside your organization. If, after they've read it, they understand what your programs do, the benefits you bring to your clients, and can feel your enthusiasm for the work, you can be confident that prospective funders will get the message as well. To the degree that your whole brain, whole heart and real soul are engaged, this gets easier.

Guiding Principle #3: Relationships

Despite the many documents and forms that funders want (and need), grantseeking depends on personal relationships and this is where your whole heart thrives. Both public and private funders will want to connect with you personally so they can get a sense of you and your organization. And yes, when you meet them, bring your brain and soul, too.

Take time to **nurture these vital relationships**. Be courteous in all of your contacts, whether in person, by telephone, via e-mail, or in print. Follow up promptly when asked for additional details. Don't annoy, but be persistent.

Nurturing relationships will be easier if you understand the funder's mission, goals, and objectives. Your interest and knowledge about them will strengthen your case and help build needed chemistry. Develop relationships with more than one person in the funding organization so you will have a safety net if your contact moves on to another job. And don't forget to nurture your existing relationships with customers or clients, board members, co-workers, and staff at other agencies and organizations—again, you never know who will give you the next fruitful lead.

Let's talk about funders for a moment. They're people, too—with the same challenges you have. They're overloaded with work, have objectives to meet, are making funding decisions based on the best available information, and are bombarded with funding requests every day at the office—and at many social events. Earn their respect, attention, and consideration with a well-organized, crisply written funding request that's brief, clear, and concise—one that stresses your *mutual* mission to improve the conditions of those in need. If they must read and reread your proposal to decipher your program, your request will likely end up in recycling.

These three guiding principles—honesty, clarity, relationships—will help your organization find the answer to practically any question related to grantseeking. For example, wondering if you should request twice the money you need in the hope that you'll get half? Consider this question in light of the three principles: Is the action honest? Does it reflect organizational clarity? Will it foster a good relationship with the funder? The answers are no, no, and no.

Honesty requires that you are able to do what you propose and that you ask for what the program needs, not for what the funder can afford to give or what you can negotiate. *Clarity* requires that your proposed idea and the results it will produce can be understood easily by those who may not be experts in your field or community. *Relationship* requires that building a solid future with your funder begins with a sincere interest in them and those you serve in partnership with them if they fund your project.

Now that we've set some guiding principles for strategic grantseeking, let's delve more specifically into the components that will make your organization stand out as one funders want to support and work with.

Chapter 2

Who Are You
and What Do You Want to Do?

Quick! Can you express your organization's vision in one brief sentence? Think of the vision statement as a slogan, sound bite or tagline that "sells" your group's mission in one quick sentence or "elevator script" (so named for the brief amount of time you have to present it). That slogan must also mesh with your organization's core values. Here are statements from two different organizations:

Our vision is that no child goes hungry.

We want every person with HIV to live a life of dignity.

Are you having trouble seeing a vision statement and making it this concise? You're not alone. Most groups are so busy serving clients and scrambling for money that they fail to spend time defining the "who-are-we?" elements needed to establish a clear vision and craft a roadmap—or mission—to accomplish it.

Doing this work at the early stage of the grantseeking process may prove to be the most important step you'll take. When everyone in your organization understands the mission clearly, they'll communicate it effectively throughout your network and, ultimately, to funders. That creates confidence and consistency in your staff, programs, and proposals.

Start by compiling key data about your organization: who it serves, what it does, where support comes from, and how you track results. You may think you already know this information, but we have found that some of the particulars may surprise you. These facts will be needed at a later stage as well, so begin collecting them now. Then, define your programs':

- Interests
- Beneficiaries
- Goals
- Desired outcomes
- Social/economic/health/educational impact
- Needs

Once you've defined these elements, compare them to each other. Do they work together logically as a whole? If not, stop and analyze what doesn't fit. Take steps now to unify all of these factors before you proceed with the proposal.

If the above elements mesh, it's time to **build a clear mission statement**. Forget about the one you wrote five years ago—or even last year. This is a fast-paced world and frequently, community needs change quickly. In fact, if you're successful, they will change. When you solve one problem, another will most certainly appear. Create a new one, from scratch, so your proposal relates to your organization's current vision and activities. Gather key people to contribute to this effort. Keep the mission statement short and meaningful—no more than one or two simple sentences.

These mission statements are built upon the vision statements set forth above:

- We are committed to improving the health of Atlanta's families through community nutrition programs, food pantries, and hunger education projects.
- Our agency assists adults in western Pennsylvania who are living with HIV-AIDS in sustaining their jobs and homes.

Next, **develop program ideas**. You may already have a list. Great! Brainstorm additional projects with your staff. (Treat them well, by the way, they are the grantwriting team you will need later). All proposed programs need to be refined through research. For each idea you consider, show how each relates to the interests, beneficiaries, goals, desired outcomes, social/economic/health/educational impact, and needs of your target community.

Find out how other organizations in your city and elsewhere are tackling similar issues. Use online search engines, databases, public agency statistics, professional publications (often found on the Web in electronic form), and networking with staff at other organizations to explore both your subject and current related projects. Funders may also have information—available in annual reports, newsletters, updates, and other material—that describes projects similar to the one you're exploring. Use this research to identify even more ideas.

Compare your ideas with others. Examine related programs and look carefully for differences. If similar projects exist in your area, be sure the one you select is an improvement, serves different needs, or widens the scope of the others. Contact the organizations that offer those programs and ask them what they're doing, who they're serving, what successes they've had, and what mistakes they've made.

Don't discourage yourself by thinking that there's not enough funding to go around, especially for similar programs. Statistics show that even when funding increases, grantseekers just don't know where to look (more about that later on).

Once you've developed an idea, evaluate how well it relates to your organization's mission and vision statements. Those themes will form the basis for your grant proposal. You must understand them and incorporate them so the proposed project follows logically from your vision and mission.

TIME FOR A GUT CHECK

Are you following your mission? Take a close look at the statement you've created. How accurately does it portray the day-to-day work of your organization? Get opinions from staff as well as from outsiders. Before going farther in grantseeking, edit your mission statement to reflect reality, or if need be, change your work to fit your mission.

Chapter 3

OK, So Where's the Money?

"Who will fund our program?" This question probably keeps you up at night. Relax, it shouldn't. There *is* funding available out there for your program. In fact, even now, in today's tough times, available funds are increasing in many areas.

So why do you feel worried and anxious about your organization's chances of landing a grant? Because of what I call a scarcity, or "zero-sum," mentality—a dispiriting belief that if one group receives funding, another one won't.

Think **abundance** instead. There's plenty of money around. In my experience, when a compelling case is made, the money shows up. Manage it well and it continues to flow.

Not flowing? Perhaps it's just not where you're looking for it. Perhaps, funders don't know enough about the needs in your field or community. Grantseeking is not only a way to identify funders, but a way to educate funders about unmet needs. In fact, many funders, and in particular government funders, base their budget requests on the nature and number of requests they receive. The more you develop good proposals, the better rationale they have for requesting funds from their source! So, don't be discouraged if some of your proposals don't get funded. Keep making the case! Help "wake up" funders to the needs of your special population or your community and show funders the value you bring in serving them.

It's easy to fall into the zero-sum trap, especially if you've got a new community to serve, have a new idea for serving them or have been turned down. It's natural to assume that funding has been cut or competition from similar programs has drained the limited pot. Don't jump to those conclusions. Instead, whether you succeed or fail, be sure to research *all* potential funders who might be interested in your proposal—not just the three or four organizations or agencies you know. Keep at it!

To find a broader universe, begin by exploring information-rich resources such as:

> **The Foundation Center:** Searches basic details on private sector funders; provides links to corporate and community foundations as well as charity grantmakers. *www.fdncenter.org*
> **Catalog of Federal Domestic Assistance:** Lists all federal agencies and their public funding grants by year and category. *www.cfda.gov*

Additionally, a comprehensive list of public and private grant resources is included in this book beginning on page 92.

Identify the type of funding opportunity—public or private—that is best suited for your proposal. It's important to do this because each type of funding requires a distinctly different method of pursuit. You'll want to match your program's interests, intentions, and needs with those of the funders you approach.

Here's a simple chart to guide you in the methods needed for success:

TYPE	THEME	HOW TO DO IT
Public funding agency	Process	Follow directions like a hawk and read everything at least twice
Private/ corporate foundation	Relationship	Develop and nurture relationships with people inside the corporation/ foundation
Corporate funds	Cause-related projects	Know the market or "cause" they care about and assure the project aligns with it

Public (government) agencies have the most money available to award and usually make the largest grants. What they expect may be summed up in three words: "Details, details, details." (Okay, so it's only one word—but it's a very important one.)

Every element of the public grantseeking process is carefully defined in the RFP application kit provided by each agency. As soon as you receive an RFP, evaluate whether your organization meets the qualifications for funding. Be sure to clarify all deadlines, documentation details (number of pages per section, size of type, etc.), and submission protocols (to whom it must be sent, where, by what date). We'll talk about that in more detail later.

Federal agency grants are tough to get and have extremely rigorous follow-up and evaluation requirements.

Private and corporate foundations are usually less rigid in their application rules, more subjective in their decision-making, and more flexible regarding the program operations of grant recipients. That said, many private funders are pleased when your organization also applies for public grants, since that shows you can comply with the more difficult governmental guidelines.

Corporations want to be good neighbors where they live and with those they serve. As a result, the Sales, Marketing, and other commercial groups have funds available to them to improve community conditions and build alliances with important groups.

Most Fortune 500 companies also have philanthropic foundations that support community efforts. These are separate from the commercially-allocated funds available to those who manage the business. Corporate foundations typically have separate governing Boards and operate with their own funds and investment portfolios. That said, corporate earnings do not necessarily determine the level of funds available from the corporate foundation.

When pursuing corporate funds, internal commercial groups should be courted separately from corporate foundations.

Corporate funds, be they from commercial groups or foundations, are the most flexible funds available. Granting cycles are not as rigid as with private foundations or government agencies, and corporate funds generally allow more flexibility with respect to program design and execution. The personal preferences of the corporate executive weighs heavily in the decision-making, and once a relationship is established and nurtured, renewing grants from year to year can become an easier process. Creating relationships here is frequently worth the effort.

When courting corporations, put yourself in their shoes and think like a business. If they decide to fund your program, what's their return-on-investment (ROI)? How will your program help meet their philanthropic objectives? Answering these questions will help you more effectively market your ideas and programs to a corporate audience. In addition to building strong community relationships, corporations want to know that their money is put to good use, so be explicit about all the benefits your ideas and programs provide.

With private funders generally, the personal relationship—not the paperwork—counts most. They like to help develop your idea. Don't show up with a "fully baked cake"—a complete plan. Instead, be patient and persistent, build a partnership with the foundation, and engage them as owners in co-designing your program.

Develop a Relationship Management Chart, as seen in this sample:

FOUNDATIONS		
SOURCE	**BACKGROUND**	**CONTACT LOG**
Apex Foundation 293 Flagler Hwy. E. Brookdale, FL 39104 **Phone**: (728) 569-9050 **Contacts:** John Parnell, Exec. Dir.; or Suresh Adami, Sr.Mgr. Contribs.	**Officers and Directors:** Roberta Q. Shuttlesworth, Pres.; Thomas Williams, V.P. and Exec. Dir.; Denise Cohen; Angel Martine, Esq.; Margaret T. Blankenhorn; Stephen Bates	**7/18:** Cheryl to identify if appropriate target, and if so, who LOI should go to. **8/16:** C. called M. Blankenhorn **9/19:** C. Met w/ Blankenhorn and Adami **10/01:** Don and C. met with Adami and Parnell; will revisit early next year

Send a two-page **Letter of Intent** (LOI) to introduce your organization. Meet with key foundation personnel several times to understand their needs and philanthropic objectives and discuss the general purpose of your idea. Use these conversations as opportunities to share information and resources as well as to solicit input on shaping the program. By the time you write the proposal, the foundation staff should know exactly what you'll be asking for—and they'll be invested in giving it life.

There are more than 70,000 corporate, family, and community foundations interested in funding worthwhile programs. Most towns, even small ones, are locations for businesses that support the community with grants. It takes time to develop relationships with them, but once you do, it's easier to get funded by them again than by public agencies.

Chapter 4

Getting There with a Little Help from Your Friends . . .

Who are your community supporters? Whether you're seeking public or private funding (or both), you need to demonstrate that your organization and its programs have enthusiastic outside support. Start collecting these endorsements now, even before creating your proposal.

Think strategically. Start by identifying the individuals, groups, and officials who already back your vision, mission or plans. From that core group, build a web of potential supporters to contact. Approach those in academic, political, professional, and community organizations related to your program focus. Look for key businesspeople, decision-makers, and opinion-setters that will bring along others—and perhaps their own expertise or financial resources—to your cause. Seek support from local government agencies and public officials.

Begin with a brief, in-person meeting to explain what your organization does. Tell stories about the needs of your community and the good things you are doing. Make it clear that there is more to do and you are ready, committed and able to do it. Follow that with on-going but simple communications to nurture the connection. Create a **chart** to help build and monitor your community relationships network.

Use your board of directors as a vital resource! Many organizations overlook how this valuable group of community leaders can mobilize other likely proponents and help conserve staff time. Brainstorm with board members to create a list of influential people they can contact. Determine who has the best access to each target and ask Board members to make those contacts.

To help them and you, **prepare a sheet of talking points to use with potential supporters.** Familiarize them with your program and solicit input about your idea. Then, **ask for written letters of endorsement** detailing precise aspects of the project and how the supporters will help those elements succeed. In fact, offer to draft those letters of support. The influential people on your target list are busy and will appreciate your providing them with a draft they can personalize. The number of letters you'll need differs with each funder, but federal agencies want as many as six. Start collecting early!

If you've been in collaborative efforts with other groups, be sure to get supportive letters from them. Funders appreciate a track record of successful alliances.

Support letters are so important that you should provide them whether your funder requires them or not. Include endorsements from agencies or foundations that have funded previous proposals. In addition, reprint key media articles, photographs, and notices that document awards your organization has won for its work or other achievements. These show that the group is a good, credible, and appreciated asset in its community.

TIME FOR A GUT CHECK

Update endorsement letters regularly. You don't want to approach a funder with support documents that are old or stale. That raises questions about how well your program has functioned recently.

Chapter 5

Oiling Your Machine

Before going much farther in grantseeking, examine your organization's internal structure. How well do individuals and departments communicate with each other? If there are rifts, work to heal them now. Establish open information exchanges—by email, phone, or in-person.

Why is this important? Too often, organizations develop program ideas—and proposals—in a vacuum. One person (or department) takes charge of the project and fails to consult others who have hands-on responsibility for putting the program into action. When a grant is awarded, there are problems—even crises—if the money doesn't match what's really needed or what actually can be delivered. I have seen projects funded for which there was insufficient internal consensus that this particular program was the priority need of the community. In the end, the group was left with a program that does not fit well and didn't work, a staff in conflict, a disappointed funder, and a blemish on its track record.

To be successful in grantseeking, your organization must not only win awards but use them well. That means thinking strategically—and yes, we hate to say it, but like a business. No one individual in any organization has all skills and information to create success in ventures today. Be sure to gather feedback on your program concept from the various staff members who will:

- Administer it
- Promote it
- Deliver it

- Be held accountable for it
- Be proud to say they were a part of it

That combined knowledge produces a stronger proposal, a more effective program, and greater likelihood the project will be funded again. Strategic planning now builds a more secure future for later.

Examine your organization's previous grant history. Ask questions of key staff members with different job functions to explore the reasons for successes and failures. Were administrative details overlooked? Was the budget unrealistic for the goals? Did you fail to monitor how well the program was actually performing? Be sure you understand—and correct—the causes of problems this time around.

Should We Team with Other Organizations?

"There's strength in numbers."

That wise saying applies to many circumstances, including grantseeking. Consider whether your group might benefit from combining efforts with several other organizations that serve similar populations with similar programs. **Coalitions or consortiums** of grantseeking groups are able to pool their collective knowledge, creating a stronger organization that's sometimes more appealing to funders.

The idea may make you nervous at first, especially if you're in a smaller agency accustomed to handling everything itself, internally, or if you have fears that you could be swallowed whole by a bigger group. The truth is, many groups, even large ones, by themselves don't have all the skills and experience necessary to mount effective projects. **Teaming up can elevate your organization to a different playing field.**

A consortium has a solid, more secure foundation than do the individual groups within it. That translates into bigger proposals, capable of winning larger awards. Consortiums are formed for grants at the federal level, where bigger is often seen as better by those who evaluate proposals.

I've seen this happen. For example, five small organizations we helped were each planning to apply for $25,000 grants. After forming a coalition, they successfully asked for $250,000 in federal funding—netting each one double what they had originally hoped to get!

Before forming a consortium, be sure to learn as much as possible about the other groups, their staff, and operations. Work out an infrastructure that everyone understands and agrees to, including the focus of the project, who will administer it, how the grant money will be distributed, what checks and balances will keep things under control, and how information will be shared.

Even if you are not part of a grantseeking consortium, remember that there's a lot to gain by working *informally* with other groups, as well. Think of them as collaborators, not competitors. Create grantwriting support groups. Get together for meetings to discuss similar programs and what's working or not. Learn from each other, so you don't waste time making others' mistakes. Encourage each other. Cheerlead! Celebrate milestones in the writing and submission process, and by all means, celebrate success. All of the groups involved and the clients they serve will benefit.

Indeed, if you avoid working with others, you may well prevent your organization from growing and maturing into a larger, more successful entity. It's been my experience that groups increase their effectiveness significantly when they work with others.

Who Creates Our Grant Proposal?

You may be accustomed to having one staff person (perhaps yourself), or an outside consultant, research and write your organization's proposals. That might work for a while. But unless you **create a team for grantseeking**, the outcome will fall short of what it could be—and might even fail.

Creating a grant proposal is like solving a jigsaw puzzle: the pieces need to fit together correctly to make it whole. The team you build should include **everyone involved in the grantseeking process**—program designers, data researchers, intake staff, those who deliver services, budget preparers, proposal writers, printing clerks and even mail room staff. The specific team members may vary slightly from project to project, and according to the size of the organization, but no one person should be solely responsible for proposal development.

Hold a proposal conference with the team early on, to talk about what needs to happen and when. This gives everyone ownership of the grantseeking process, which in turn promotes creativity, enthusiasm, careful attention to details and the opportunity to enhance the network that leads to funding. Of course, certain people will have larger roles in designing and writing the proposal, but all team members need to understand the big picture and communicate it whenever they get the chance.

Accomplish these tasks at the initial proposal meeting:

- Set up a calendar of all critical deadlines;
- Brainstorm major themes and implementation issues;
- Identify who is responsible for what information;
- Set deadlines for when information is due;
- Create an editorial review committee; and
- Schedule the next full team meeting for progress updates.

Input from others builds more than just a successful grant application—it helps your program succeed.

Some organizations have a grantwriter on staff, or rely on someone in the business development or accounting department to write the proposal. If these people don't connect with the staff actually delivering services, disaster can occur. I've seen it happen: a proposal was funded for the requested amount, but the hands-on staff couldn't provide the promised level of services. This led to a dismal chain-reaction: the program did not achieve its goals . . . staff worked unrealistically hard . . . to the point of burn-out . . . and fewer clients were served well.

Think it will take too much time to organize a team or that your organization doesn't have enough staff to make it meaningful? Even a two-person operation can benefit from thinking and acting like a team. In fact, even one person, working alone in a start-up organization should seek out a team of people to help them! The time taken in a meeting or two in the beginning will more than pay off in the final result. Sticking with your team all way to the finish line will enhance your chances of success.

Oh, and back to the mail clerk. If you think that person isn't important, think again. I've seen large grant proposals be refused funding due to the tardiness of the submission (not 3 days late, but 3 minutes late!), lacking appropriate attachment documents, and the general sloppiness that accompanies proposals pulled together at the eleventh hour without team collaboration.

LESSONS LEARNED
Better communication, early on, supports success!

Chapter 6

Producing a Winning Proposal Every Time

Experience does not matter. Whether this is your first proposal or you've been winning grants for years, you can succeed! To enhance your chances, get to know and follow the requirements set forth by the grantmaker. Yes, those details are often tedious to read, sometimes hard to follow, and always time—consuming to carry out, but do so and you'll sleep better at night. Ignore them and your proposal will be rejected outright.

Know the Requirements

If you're applying for a federal grant, get the RFP (Request for Proposal) *and* the application kit (if one is offered) from the agency. Agencies go to great lengths to compile application kits that clarify what they want in the proposal, yet many grantseekers overlook this helpful, important material.

When you have this information, **read it over three times** before you call the agency with questions about the RFP. Fielding questions that are addressed in the application kit annoys agency grant managers. Follow all guidelines or application instructions. These are not suggestions—they're rules! Don't pick and choose among them. As you read, **highlight every requirement.** Then, check back as you write the proposal, and check again when the proposal is completed to make sure you've conformed to each detail.

Government agencies are especially strict in enforcing requirements for number of pages, type size (varies by font style), and even the space allowed between lines of type. Don't ignore those details.

Private and corporate foundations and funders may have fewer rules for what proposals should look like, but be sure to read all instructions carefully anyway because they specify details that should not be overlooked. Following the discipline imposed by federal agencies will make your group look sharp and capable as you approach the private sector.

One of the best ways to make sure that your proposal meets every requirement is to create a **compliance matrix**—that's a fancy term for a checklist. In many cases, the RFP will include a list of required elements. If it doesn't, it's well worth the time to make one. Simply go through the RFP, list all the requirements (they will be easy to find if you highlighted them!), and put a line or box next to each so you can check it off as you complete that part of the proposal. **Double-check your proposal against the compliance matrix before you submit it.**

Length

Your proposal—and each of its parts—must conform to the required length as stated in the RFP. Reviewers read as many as 20 proposals a day, and some look for a quick way to disqualify candidates. A proposal that exceeds the page limit may end up on the rejection pile before it has been read, regardless of how good it is.

Set margins to a standard measure. Don't reduce them in an attempt to increase the number of words per page. It will be noticed, and not appreciatively.

Type

The number of letters that fit per line is determined by both the font (typeface style) and point size of the type you choose. Most people find it easier to read a *serif* font style (such as Times New

Roman) than a *sans serif* font (such as Arial). Set a goal to make the proposal visually pleasing and comfortable for the reader. If type size and style are not stated in the grant instructions, use *Times New Roman 12-point type* for best readability. Figures and tables may use smaller type sizes, depending upon RFP requirements, but the text must be readable.

Format

Outlines, section headings, or questions mentioned in the RFP or application must be presented in the order indicated. Be sure to respond to each fully.

Keep your proposal short, simple, and well-organized and it will be easy for the reviewer to read (and love!). Condense details and tighten prose. If the text is so long you are tempted to reduce the margins to make it fit, let the proposal sit unread for two or three days. When you re-read it with fresh eyes, you'll see where the text can be tightened.

Every grant proposal you submit should be a fresh creation, even if it's for a project you've tried to get funded elsewhere. Even if you already know this funder, view every new proposal as the start of a new relationship. Through your research and personal contacts, learn about the funder's objectives and requirements and then tailor your request according to what you have learned. Don't dust off generic, boilerplate documents and send them to prospective funders.

Language

Use writing that is clear, concise, and grammatically correct, including proper punctuation. Don't use long or complicated sentences. Keep paragraphs short and clear. Flowery language makes it difficult for the reviewer to read and comprehend what you are saying, and hurts your program's chances of being funded.

State your goals and project plan in a forthright, positive way. To accomplish this, use the active rather than the passive voice. When discussing expected outcomes, describe what the project <u>will</u> do. Avoid conditional words such as "if," "could," or "might," which create the sense that your organization is unsure of itself, the project, and the proposal.

Choose words that echo your organizational and programmatic themes. Build alliances by referring to potential funders or donors as partners, friends, or supporters. Instead of saying what your group "needs" from a funding source, speak to the "opportunities" to "partner" with that agency or foundation.

Provide the facts and statistical data about your project and be sure those numbers are correct. Then, let your passion show. Use your proposal to convey the spirit of your organization and its commitment to the community.

Assume that the person reading the proposal knows little about your program, your organization, or even your field. **Use clear, explanatory language** to help the reader connect the dots between a problem in the community and your solution.

Avoid acronyms (ROI, NGO, CSO), insider terms and phrases ("shooting gallery"), or overworked buzzwords ("mission-critical"), —all of which make your content either hard to understand, tiresome to read . . . or both!

Components

No matter how much experience you have, writing a proposal nearly always seems overwhelming at the beginning. To make the task more manageable, break it down into smaller segments and tackle one segment at a time, rewarding yourself along the way.

While specific components may vary according to grantor requirements, in general, the proposal package should include:

- 501(c)(3) tax exemption certification letter for your organization

- Cover Letter*
- Title Page
- Table of Contents*
- Proposal Summary*
- Introduction of Organization*
- Problem Statement and Needs Assessment*
- Project Objectives*
- Project Methods and Design*
- Project Evaluation*
- Budget and Personnel*
- Other Funding*
- Independent audit statements
- Letter signed by CEO of national organization, verifying your group as local affiliate or chapter (if applicable)
- Memorandum of agreement or support letter from current partner/collaborator organizations

Additional supporting documents that are not required, but are usually wise to provide, include:

- List of board members, including their employers and titles
- Organization's overall budget for latest fiscal year
- Brochure used for educational or development purposes
- Recent issue of group's newsletter
- Copy of latest annual report
- Long-term plan for organization, or list of annual goals
- Letters of support

DISCUSSED IN DETAIL
*These items are discussed in detail in Chapter 7, **Grantwriting Guide-Basic Tools & Tips**.

TIME FOR A GUT CHECK

Before starting to write, filter all elements of your planned proposal through the three guiding principles:

- *Honesty*
- *Clarity*
- *Relationships*

Have you kept on target with these? If not, it will be easier to make the changes now—not after you've written the proposal.

FIRST THINGS LAST

Although the Cover Letter, Table of Contents, and Proposal Summary appear at the front of your submission—and are discussed here in that sequence—they should not be written until the proposal text is completed That's the only way to be sure you've accurately chosen the key highlights of your plan.

Chapter 7

Grantwriting Guide: Basic Tools & Tips

Think of this section as a professional course in the fundamentals of writing a grant proposal. In it, you'll find the help you need to build a winning document, step-by-step. We've described each proposal element separately, to help you understand what it is and how to create it.

In addition to *telling* you how to present your program's case effectively, we'll *show* you as well. Excerpts of writing samples (with fictitious identifying information) are included as attachments at the back of this handbook to demonstrate good techniques.

Read this section thoroughly before starting your preliminary research. Consult it again as you create the first draft of your proposal and, later, when polishing the final product.

Cover Letter

What It Is: Think of this as the card that accompanies a gift. Keep it short, sweet, and direct.

What to Include: **Just the basics**—who is sending the proposal, who is receiving it, and no more than two lines thanking the person for the opportunity to submit the proposal. Do not describe your program idea here.

How to Build It: Write the cover letter after you've completed all revisions of the proposal itself. The letter should be signed by the most senior executive or administrator in your organization. Triple-check the spelling, especially the spelling of all names. An error in the cover letter will stand out and will erode confidence in the proposal.

Table of Contents

What It Is: **A title and page number list** for every section of the proposal is recommended for any proposal containing more than five pages.

What to Include: Section names, appendices by title, itemized attachments—all with corresponding page numbers.

How to Build It: Compile the Table of Contents after the proposal has been revised and all supplementary documents collected. Mark up a copy of the packet, highlighting each element to be included in the Table of Contents.

Proposal Summary

What It Is: A well-written, **compelling snapshot of your program's main elements**, the summary is the funder's first impression of your organization. An effective summary entices reviewers to continue reading and is critical to successful grantseeking. It is the platform on which the proposal is built.

What to Include: Note **each key factor**, compelling or creative aspect of your program, and objectives. Emphasize how the project is unique, different, or more effective than others—whether it's targeting specific populations, meeting a special need, or using innovative methods.

How to Build It: Write the summary after the main proposal is completed. Review the entire text, highlight key points, and use those points to develop a summary.

Introduction of the Organization

What It Is: The "getting-to-know-us" section builds reviewer confidence in your group, its efforts, and the people who run it. The **aim is to establish credibility** and show how well the organization qualifies for the funding offered. Succeed here and the grantmaker will see the benefits of long-term partnerships with you.

What to Include: Begin by describing your organization's philosophy. Use key data about the group and its current operations, as well as a review of past programs, to show how that philosophy drives your actions.

Demonstrate your ability to work with other organizations by describing your track record with other grantors. List exceptional results and successes.

Discuss past work and successes with your target groups for this project's proposal. If this proposal targets a new population or heads in a new direction, describe past work that demonstrates your ability to "bridge" to this new venture. Describe the services you want to offer and the financial, material, and human resources your organization currently has to meet those needs.

Provide information and data that relate to the funder's goals. If you've won awards, or received media attention for meritorious work, or if any clients or staff can claim such achievements, this is the time to say so to build your credibility.

Include *brief* **biographies of board members and key staff people**. Show how your board members' community leadership enhances your organization and makes its programs more effective.

How to Build It: **Review** program evaluations, annual reports, and current operational plans. **Confer** with service delivery staff as well as administrators about past successes and resources available for the proposed program.

Request updated biographies from board members and organization staff, complete with professional/work affiliations and titles. Summarize each in a sentence or two. Put complete biographies at the end of the document, as attachments.

Problem Statement and Needs Assessment

What It Is: A forthright and well-supported presentation of the need or problem that your program will address. This key section must thoroughly, yet concisely, **establish the case** for the project you are proposing.

What to Include: All factual information directly related to the problem as you see it. Use historic, geographic, and quantitative data, as well as studies by other groups, reports, critiques, and surveys.

Define the needs of the service area and target population, showing how the problem affects those you intend to serve and the greater community-at-large. Provide summaries of your own data to show how your organization has provided help and to document unmet needs.

Avoid making assumptions or using unverified assertions that aren't backed-up with data. Be sure to use any relevant data that the funder—whether government agency or foundation—has collected or published.

Anecdotes—stories of the people you serve and their experiences—help illustrate the data findings. These should come from your organization's work. Use the voices of the people you serve to connect the heart of the reader with the proposed plan and convey why your organization cares.

Include a **description of the resources needed,** how those funds will be used, positive outcomes expected, and post-funding plans for sustaining the project and its results. Be realistic about grant-review and award timeframes. Funders commonly require two to twelve months to process grant applications. Your requests must account for funding delays, or, if special circumstances require, make a clear case for an expedited funding decision.

How to Build It: Grant reviewers want to see the **facts**. If you're short on data, especially about the target service area or population, students and faculty at area colleges may be willing to help gather statistics, perform literature searches, and conduct field interviews to obtain the data you need. In addition to being efficient, linking to academia can help build credibility.

Naturally, creating data takes time. If you're going this route, think ahead and allow sufficient time—at least six months—to create and **conduct a survey**. Be sure the researcher understands what data you need, how it should be collected, in what format, and by what deadlines. If your target population has special needs or cultural sensitivities, be sure the research team knows about them. Although this will be a time-consuming process, valid and reliable data can be used again and again in seeking a variety of grants and may be well worth the effort.

It is a rare group that does not already have internal data, but many have not yet organized that data to their best advantage. This occurs because previous funders have asked for reports that satisfy their own internal reporting requirements, rather than the operating realities of projects in the field. Analyzing old reports for new ways to present information may help you reconfigure the data into more compelling stories and usable formats.

If you have a wealth of information, eliminate anything that doesn't relate directly to the purpose of this project. Organize material so that this section presents evidence of the problem and its consequences at personal, local, and national levels. **Focus the data on the target of this project and the funder's interests.** If special surveys were conducted, document how the data was collected.

Follow the data with your organization's proposed solution, and demonstrate to the funder that there is a good match between the problem you have described and the project you are proposing. Avoid the temptation to overstate the problem or dramatize it to the point that it seems unsolvable. **Emphasize the opportunities** inherent in your project and show why it is vital for the target community. Show confidence in your organization, the proposed project, and its funding success.

Project Objectives

What It Is: Description of your proposed program's **activities, goals, and desired outcome**.

What to Include: Objectives that tie directly to the needs you described in the problem statement and needs assessment. State how you plan to achieve these goals. Discuss every segment of the target population, how they will be chosen and served, and the outcome or results expected.

Do not include the methods you will use to achieve the objectives of the project—that discussion comes in the next section.

How to Build It: The objectives and goals must proceed logically from the problem statement and needs assessment. If your objectives contain statistically measurable results, these should be believable, realistic, understandable, and verifiable. Results—like projects—should be based on what you know is best and want to do, not on what you think the funder wants to hear.

Confer with your team and assure that service delivery staff and administrators **create objectives that will be attainable with the funds you are requesting**. Develop objectives that accurately reflect your project plan and budget. Don't over-promise. Promise what you know you can deliver based on your experience, track record, and lessons learned. Too many organizations under-deliver and erode trust with their funders because they promise too much and request too little. There is no risk in setting big goals if the organization can inspire confidence, the project plan is sound, and the budget can support it.

Remember: if your proposal is funded, the objectives cited in this section will be used to evaluate your program's progress and success, which may well determine if you will receive funding for subsequent projects.

Project Methods and Design

What It Is: The **blueprint** of your program. This plan of action shows how the proposed program is expected to work and solve the target problem.

What to Include: **All planned activities, resources needed, and staff requirements**. Highlight innovative features that distinguish your organization's plan from others.

This section is the "nuts and bolts" of your proposed program, explained in enough detail that funders will know all the requirements—whether people, space, or office equipment. If data is used, mention only what is relevant and what has been previously cited, since new data will be confusing.

Use flow charts or tables to describe the organization and management of the project, showing its structure, interrelationships, staff responsibilities and deployment, facilities, transportation needed, and necessary support services.

Diagram the program to help explain its scope and detail. For example, show activities in three stages: **Input** ("five social workers identify clients"), **Throughput** ("two nurses counsel clients") and **Output** ("25 informed adults weekly"). Be specific about time frames and how the program will meet them.

Supporting details should be provided in the Appendix. These give the reviewer immediate access to data, but may detract from the readability of the proposal, so choose them wisely. Appropriate material for the appendix includes:

• supplementary data references

- information needing in-depth analysis
- timetables, work plans, schedules, activities
- methodologies
- legal documents
- resumes or curricula vitae of proposed staff
- letters of support, endorsements

How to Build It: It will be easier to develop this section of the proposal if you remove yourself mentally and emotionally from the proposed program. Sometimes we know too much to describe the details clearly enough for those who are not intimately involved or already committed to our cause. Be methodical and complete. Think through and describe **every task and step** involved, by each project staff member. If it's required to run the project effectively, include it here.

Construct a clear, specific set of directions, written as if the reader has no background in your field. Imagine that person has been given full responsibility for starting the proposed program. Create the blueprint needed for guidance, including visuals such as flow charts. This effort will pay off in the long run. If you're funded, this section of the proposal can provide essential guidance for the person who is assigned or hired to run the project.

Project Evaluation

What It Is: The **plan for demonstrating results**. Evaluations describe and judge. They show how the program was implemented, whether it was consistent with its design, and what impact it produced. It compares the results with the promises in the proposal, explains failures and successes, and captures lessons learned.

What to Include: **Whatever is needed for a thorough project assessment**, including the amount of time needed, how objectives will be benchmarked, mechanisms for distributing feedback to staff, the schedule for review and comment, the cost of writing and communicating the results, and the funding required to conduct the evaluation.

Specify how and when the project will be evaluated. The strongest programs include an evaluation design in the proposal, collect evaluation data during operations, and use that data for mid-course corrections. Even if a funder specifies certain evaluation techniques, don't hesitate to add your organization's techniques as well.

State whether an **outside evaluator** will be used. A third-party assessment of your program shows organizational confidence. Independent evaluators also provide valuable information for increasing program effectiveness, and funders are often willing to support the costs of outside evaluators.

How to Build It: Funders need evaluations, but your organization needs them even more. Evaluation is vital to both program success and organizational longevity. Properly framed and conducted, it will support and sustain your group's future success.

If there's an RFP, read it carefully and **incorporate any evaluation tools stipulated by the funder**. If the funder does not specify evaluation tools, describe the ones your organization will use and state when and how frequently the funder will receive reports.

Allow enough time for your objectives to be accomplished. Things inevitably take longer than planned.

Design the evaluation to **measure outcomes**, including return on investment (ROI) and program impact as well as the sheer numbers of people served. Some organizations think the best evaluation is one that shows an increase in the number of people being served, but that's not true if those clients aren't being served well.

Project Budget

What It Is: A **full detailing of the proposed project's expenses** and what the requested grant will cover. The budget must be consistent with the overall proposal narrative and appropriate for the program's objectives and methods.

What to Include: **Salaries, equipment, and supplies** are the most obvious, but there are other expenses as well.

It's easy to forget some of the invisible expenses. Be sure to consider the costs of leases, evaluation systems, matching requirements, audits, development, and the creative or maintenance fees for information and accounting systems. If you plan to hire new staff for the project, remember to include the additional space and equipment that will be required to support them.

Indirect costs are acceptable, but they are often subject to close scrutiny by grant reviewers. They include utilities, rental of buildings and equipment, projected salary increases, food, telephones, insurance, and transportation.

Bulk rate postage and printing costs are appropriate budget items if your project will conduct public outreach through mass mailings. Don't incorporate trivial amounts for postage, letterhead, photocopying, and similar items if not essential to project operations, however. Funders may perceive those expenses as part of normal operating costs and negatively infer the proposal budget has been artificially inflated.

Reasonable training and consultant costs are acceptable, but many foundations are watchful for over-inflated figures in this category as well. Their reasoning is simple: If your staff has the expertise to perform program activities, why do they need to attend out-of-state seminars or be trained by outside consultants? In this fast-changing world, there may be good reasons why you need training and consultants, just be sure to describe why this is the case.

Be cautious about travel-related line items, especially for program proposals intended to only have local impact. If attending a distant conference is vital for project effectiveness, justify it in the budget narration.

Pilot projects may show a contingency line item if appropriate. Be explicit about those expenses and give examples.

Do not include any general miscellaneous items in the budget. Even small expenses should be allocated to their proper categories.

Use the budget to **reflect your organization's values** as well as your fiscal good sense. An AIDS program, for example, may want to hire HIV-positive individuals for positions instead of staffing the project exclusively with paid staff who are not affected by HIV.

The budget period you show must not exceed the maximum award period allowed by the grantor. Otherwise, a reviewer might think your organization is unable or unwilling to complete the proposed work in the required time frame.

If certain active or pending items in your budget are funded by other sources, list the source of these funds with the appropriate item.

How to Build It: Prepare the budget after the rest of the proposal is complete. That way, every aspect of the project—from rent to staffing to evaluation—will be clearly defined.

Be sure that your budget is realistic. **Conduct a thorough, internal assessment of what it will really cost** to operate the program as described. Ask for that amount. Don't ask for twice as much in hopes of receiving half. Similarly, don't ask for too little, keeping your fingers crossed that—maybe—you'll be able to do it for less.

Pay staff what they deserve and reflect that in the budget. Don't undercut their value because they are committed to the project or doing work that is socially good. Doing good may provide satisfaction, but it does not buy the groceries. If you underpay, sooner or later you'll lose good staff. Do not depend on volunteers or overworked staffers to run the proposed program. They will burn out, and the project, the organization, your funding relationships, and your reputation will suffer.

Do sufficient research to estimate costs and related expenses. If the grant needs to fund a vehicle, you need to know what maintenance, insurance, and gas will cost.

Focus your details on the **cost-benefit ratio** of the proposed program. Show how your budget will get the most out of the grantor's dollars. Emphasize the value of the project's long-term benefits and how the grant will leverage other funding.

Use specific detail to identify line items within budget categories and provide justification for those items in the narrative. A grant reviewer may reduce the funds recommendation if one of these two elements is missing. This can happen, for example, if consultant costs are included without describing that person's role in the project or expensive equipment appears in the budget with no justification for its use.

Be sure that your budget is consistent. Salaries for the proposed program and those for the organization's current positions should be similar. Check for consistency between the project description, proposal narrative, and budget line items. When your budget is completed, a reviewer should be able to examine it item by item and find each element discussed in the narrative.

Account for any unusual budget increases or decreases. Likewise, if your budget includes a line item that was not previously requested, explain it fully.

Create management efficiency. If your Executive Director position is funded through a government contract, five percent of that person's time might be allocated to oversee this project, at no extra cost. Recruit a board member or other expert to donate services (such as training or financial advice), and include this in the budget as an in-kind contribution.

Identify the percentage of each staff member's time that will be spent on the project, then pro-rate the costs. For employees whose salaries are paid in full by another source, show the percentage paid as a contribution from that source. Do not ask the funder to pay for salaries that are covered elsewhere.

Obtain exact cost information for fringe benefits and payroll taxes from your human resources department or payroll service.

If practical, explore whether your program could share major pieces of equipment with other nonprofit organizations or purchase reliable used items.

Funding levels in federal assistance programs change yearly. Review what's been appropriated over the past several years in order to project future funding levels. Multi-year proposals should include an inflation factor and projected salary increases.

Use restraint in determining inflationary cost projections. Anticipate possible future increases, but don't pad budget line items.

Never anticipate that the income from the grant you're applying for will be the sole support for the project.

Apportion the funding request carefully. No more than 40% of the grant should be slated for personnel, with 60% earmarked for direct program support.

Funding sources usually specify what percentage of the project's cost must come from **matching funds or in-kind contributions** from the organization submitting the proposal or a third party. Private foundations prefer a designated cash match. Government funders may allow the fair market value of furniture, computers, equipment, and a percentage of office space as part of the required nonprofit match. Remove contributions to any matching fund from the budget (if matching costs are required), unless application instructions state otherwise.

Dollar amounts should be shown in whole numbers—do not include cents. Correct form is $1,270 (not 1270).

If there are multiple funders, use separate columns to show the amount each is underwriting.

Future Funding

What It Is: **Long-term planning** for continuing the project beyond the grant period. No grantor wants to feel as if it will be the perpetual funder of an organization or program, so describe a plan for developing sustained financial support from elsewhere. Showing that the organization is planning for the future gives the program professionalism and credibility.

What to Include: **Realistic plans** to keep the program running when initial funding ends. If the funding covers construction, discuss maintenance and the availability of future program grants and other resources for implementing services.

When the funding covers equipment purchases, account for necessary on-going expenditures. For example, if a grant has been used to buy a vehicle, future costs will include insurance, gas, maintenance, and parking.

Detail your organization's long-term vision, strategic thinking, and staff capabilities for finding matching funds from other sources. Show how project growth will be supported.

How to Build It: Conduct a thorough internal assessment of on-going needs and costs. Be forthright about what it will take to keep the program operational, even if you fear funder "sticker shock."

Use internal data to inform projections for needs.

Identify prospective source types (such as private foundations or public agencies) for future funding objectives. Structure sources and their potential grants within specific years going forward.

Consider the timeframe of the current proposal. Many organizations fail to account for how inflationary costs—rent, wages, and benefits, to name just a few—will eat away at an initial grant amount. Factor those into your future picture.

Portray your organization as a catalyst that inspires other groups, rather than as a perpetual funding drain. Discuss where you see the program going. It's fine to undertake a pilot project, because that shows funders you want to fine-tune an idea on a small scale before asking for a large grant. Talk about what **changes in staff or activities** might happen between the pilot stage and the future program—and how funding needs will increase.

Attachments or Appendix

What It Is: Supplementary material placed at the end of the proposal that explains, supports, enlarges upon, and illustrates the narrative.

What to Include: Relevant and appropriate charts, tables, photographs, research documents, studies, media coverage, evidence of collaborative efforts, testimonials, awards, and letters of support.

How to Build It: Collect data for charts and other research materials as you prepare the proposal narrative. Ask your staff for news articles and testimonials about your organization, its programs, and community efforts. Consult with your board of directors and staff for contacts in political, civic, business, and social welfare circles who might write meaningful, supportive letters about the proposed project and its importance.

DISCUSSED IN DETAIL
See Online Funding Resources.

TIME FOR A GUT CHECK

If you have previously submitted a Letter of Intent (LOI) to a private funder, review it now. Make sure that the proposal you're about to write reflects the description of the project in the LOI. If the project idea has changed substantively, even through collaborative discussions with the funder, send a follow-up LOI before you start to write. Private and corporate foundations expect to know what you'll be requesting, and why, in advance of receiving the formal proposal.

Once you have completed a first draft of the proposal, read it over to see how well each section reflects the three guiding principles of Honesty, Clarity, and Relationships. Edit any changes or additions into your second draft before the editorial review process begins.

BONUS BENEFIT

Preparing the "Future Funding" section can establish a jumping-off point for your organization to begin searching for funds in new places. There are many more agencies and foundations providing funds for your type of services than the grantors you tradition—ally approach. Once you've completed the internal assessment of your program's on-going needs, start seeking new prospective funders.

Chapter 8

Effective Editing with Fresh Eyes

You've done the research, written the narrative, and compiled the charts. All you need to do now is send it off, right? No! You need to build enough time into your grantwriting schedule for a thorough edit of the entire package—application, proposal, and attachments.

To avoid creating a patchwork document, which often happens when a proposal is written by a group, have one person do the final write-through to **smooth the flow** before editing.

Having a well-edited proposal is vital to funding success. Your group's passion for its service and the project's good intentions cannot make up for a poorly written document. Spelling and grammatical mistakes reflect negatively on your organization. So do wordiness, jargon, redundancies, misplaced pages, inaccurately labeled material, and more. A good editor scrutinizes prose, page numbers, type fit, titles, names, and numbers.

Edit to hold the reader's interest and make the proposal easy to understand. Change high-brow words into simple ones. Turn the passive voice into an active one. Break long sentences into several smaller ones. Avoid mind-numbing blocks of type by controlling paragraph lengths. Organize material in logical, related units if no specific order is required. **Proofread carefully** for spelling and other errors. Check that all requirements from the grantor have been fulfilled.

You may want to have a knowledgeable staff person read the proposal for substance, but you **must** have a pair of "**fresh**

eyes"—someone who hasn't helped develop, write or review the proposal drafts—to edit the final manuscript. That person is better able to catch mistakes, see problems, improve continuity, and increase clarity than those who helped with the grantwriting itself. Should you use an outside editor? If the program is important to your organization and it's a large, multi-year grant, you may want to.

"But I have a spell-check on my computer," you're thinking. "Why do I need an editor?" While a spellcheck program can find many spelling and grammatical mistakes, it can't discern when a correctly spelled word is inappropriate for the sentence—as in, "It took many daze to right hour proposal." Spell-check won't know that James Johnson should really be Jane Jonson, or if a wordy sentence ought to be cut. All those decisions, and more, take human judgment.

If co-workers are reviewing several drafts of the proposal, edit each version, including the final one. Decide who will incorporate committee comments, respond to critiques, and make decisions about what information goes into the proposal.

As a final step, ask someone outside your organization to "score" the proposal for you, just as the funder might. If they find any weaknesses, don't despair. Just make the corrections now, and get yet another good night's sleep.

Chapter 9

Details, Details, Details

You've worked hard on the content of the proposal, but there is a rule of thumb about projects like this: the last 5% of what you do is the first 95% that funders see.

In other words, packaging makes an impression. Take as much care in deciding how the proposal will look and how it will be delivered to the funder as you did in creating its substance.

Print, collate, copy, and package the proposal **neatly and according to the funder's instructions**. Some grantors require special procedures for printing, wrapping, or mailing.

Make as many copies as requested, plus several extras for your own reference. Inspect each copy for uniformity. **Double-check to be sure** all elements, including every attachment, are in the proposal package before mailing. Once your proposal gets to a funder, there's no one there to be your advocate, apologize for any mistakes, or find missing pages.

Check proposal requirements to see if specific binding is requested. If none is specified, bind proposals either with clamps or hard covers. Do not use staples or spiral binding, which make it difficult to photocopy your submission for committee review.

Mail early enough for the proposal to reach its destination by the deadline, but no more than four days in advance. Don't submit it so early that it looks as if you merely dusted off a proposal that was prepared for a previous attempt and sent it in with no thought of the specific requirements of this funder. Some agencies have receipt-date stipulations for judging whether a proposal is on time, such as the postmark or delivery date. Check with the grantor if you have any questions.

Consult the instructions for the **correct name and title** of the person to whom the proposal should be sent. Double-check that the mailing label has the correct name and address. Your organization has a lot to lose if your package goes astray due to preparation errors, so it's well worth checking and re-checking these details.

Even the way you send the proposal to the grantor is important. Restrain the impulse to use a premium courier service, such as Federal Express. Although that's a minor expense compared to the significance of the proposal to your organization, many grantors see overnight shipping as a waste of limited funds and may worry about how efficiently your organization will use the resources they provide for program costs.

You can achieve the same reassurance that your proposal arrived safely by sending it via U.S. Priority Mail, with delivery tracking and confirmation. Be sure to check delivery tracking online to confirm that the package has arrived.

If you learn that your proposal did not arrive at its destination by the required deadline due to a mistake on the part of the courier, you may attempt to explain the cause of delay to your grantor immediately and in writing. However, only do so if you have a paper trail that **verifies you submitted the document to the courier in a timely manner**. Unfortunately, public sector funders will not likely accept your proposal if it is late, regardless of the cause for tardiness, but it's worth trying to explain yourself given all the work that you've invested in the proposal itself. Private sector funders may be more lenient, but don't count on it.

Chapter 10

What Now?

Three words: patience, patience, **patience!** Waiting for an answer can seem endless, but in reality, the average wait is only six to eight weeks. Once you've mailed the proposal, find something else important to do.

In the private sector, it's okay to make **one follow-up phone call, about four weeks after submission.** This call should be placed by the person in your organization who signed the proposal's cover letter. Call the person designated on the grant application or RFP. Use the call to verify receipt of the proposal, suggest an in-person meeting to further discuss the planned project, determine whether the review process has begun (and, if so, what stage it's at), and find out when a decision might occur.

Do not make more than one call, unless the funder has given you specific approval to do so. Multiple post-submission calls are intrusive and annoying. Reviewers may feel you're being pushy, and over-eagerness sends a signal that the organization may be financially unsound and dependent upon this funding.

If you haven't heard anything for several weeks after the decision date, or for more than four months after submitting the proposal, then placing another call is advisable.

For publicly funded grants, do not call. Check your shipment tracking service to learn when the proposal was received. The only time to call a public sector grantor is if they've posted a notice online

51

stating that grantees have been announced, but your organization hasn't received any response.

Stay positive. The process takes time. Allow it to work.

Guess Who's Coming to Visit?

In some cases, the grantor will request a site visit while a proposal is under review. If your organization receives such a request, don't panic. It usually means your proposal is close to being approved. Funders say there's an 80% chance your program will be approved after a site visit. In my experience, the chances of approval are closer to 98%!

So, relax. Then make sure your whole organization looks professional for the visit. Prepare thoroughly. Re-read the proposal. **Alert everyone who will be involved in the program to be on-site** for the visit and ready to answer questions. If your staff usually wears casual clothing to work, do what works for your organization and allow them to do so that day, as long as "casual" does not mean "sloppy." Appearance does matter. The staff needs to look like they can handle the funds, after all. People who look casual can inspire that confidence, people who look sloppy, can't.

Be ready to conduct a tour of the premises and any auxiliary areas. Make an advance plan to determine which staff members will be responsible for what duties, including hosting the visit, conducting meetings, providing transportation to other sites (if appropriate), and providing coffee breaks, snacks, and lunches.

After the site visit, be sure to send a thank-you note to all those from the funding source who attended the site visit.

We Won!

If you receive the requested grant, send a thank-you letter immediately to the agency or foundation. Then send similar notes to staff, supporters, and others who helped your organization in the grantseeking effort.

Take steps now to **develop and enhance relationships** with grantor staff. These alliances will help sustain your program and facilitate the funding of future projects.

Construct a timetable showing when the funds will be received, the anticipated start date for the program, when reports to the grantor need to be filed, and so on. Go beyond what's required and **send the grantor regular, substantive updates** about the project and its accomplishments. Extend personal invitations to visit the project site.

If appropriate, notify community and professional publications about the award and the project it will fund. This is a good way to build awareness, on-going interest, and lay the groundwork for future grants.

We Lost!

You've gotten bad news—now what? As above, your first action should be sending a thank-you note. Express your organization's appreciation that the grantor took the time to review the proposal. Thanking them shows that you're a good player, and one they might be happy to hear from again. A note also creates another contact, which helps build the relationship for the future.

Turn the loss into constructive action. **Find out why** your request was denied. Was the proposal late or incomplete? Was the project idea too narrow, poorly researched, or poorly written? Was this the appropriate funder? Did the reviewer think your organization lacked the ability to run what sounded like a good program? Did the grantor have insufficient funds to underwrite your project?

The reasons for not being funded are wide and varied. You need to know, specifically, which were relevant to your proposal, and learn from that feedback. Send a polite letter requesting reviewer comments and suggestions for future submissions. Although some grantors may not have the staff resources to provide such feedback, many do. They often score each section of the proposal, showing areas of strength and weakness. Be persistent about getting this information.

Uncovering why the proposal was turned down will be enormously important to your future grantseeking efforts. You'll be able to incorporate that feedback into revisions of this proposal or new plans for other projects. Indeed, in the long run, finding out why your proposal was rejected may prove to be more valuable than receiving approval on your initial attempt would have been.

TIME FOR A GUT CHECK

After 25 percent of your grant period has been completed, compare what your program is delivering to what your proposal said it would do. Measure its short-term outcomes against the three guiding principles—Honesty, Clarity, Relationships—and take steps to make needed adjustments quickly.

Chapter 11

You've Got Momentum, Don't Stop!

Now that the grantseeking cycle is completed, it's tempting to put the proposal on the shelf until the next funding deadline looms. Don't do it! Instead, think of your organization's grantseeking efforts as a continuously running machine that you must oil and maintain for optimal performance.

Work towards sustainability. End eleventh-hour planning, research, and writing by developing proposal information in an on-going vision of what the program and organization can do. Then, instead of relying on funding that takes a crisis-driven, year-by-year or program-by-program approach, you'll have a long-term strategy in place to create a reliable income stream.

If you're receiving a public grant, begin researching how you can target the private sector for matching funds to sustain the program or increase its scope. Especially with private funders, make the time to develop and nurture grantseeking relationships. Remember to be patient, as private sector relationships can take 1-2 years of nurturing before they bear fruit.

Now is also the time to build consortiums—alliances with other organizations and groups working in the same field. Collaborations please funders and can be very productive and profitable for your organization, given the right mix of groups, individuals, and resources.

Explore ways your program can become a catalyst for others. That solidifies the importance of your organization, increases the number of projects providing service, and benefits more people.

Outcomes and evaluations are becoming more valuable. These measures should be *as* important, if not *more* important, to your organization as they are to your funder. You need to assess the impact of your program, how many people have been served, how well they've been served, and the return on investment (ROI). Having such data supports on-going funding, builds your organization's reputation, and creates the institutional memory necessary to prepare subsequent proposals.

Whether your funds have a public or private source, you should set up internal and external systems for accountability and evaluation. These will record the data for measuring program successes and alert you when the program is not functioning correctly.

Public agencies provide painstakingly specific evaluation techniques. If you find that the required methods actually impede the functioning of your program and are more onerous than those of other public agencies, let the grantor know. Identify other recipients of the same grant and find out if they share your views. If so, write a letter to the public agency stating your views and have it signed by all recipients of the grant. You'd be amazed at the impact of collective letters. Remember that your funder may not realize their evaluation techniques are unnecessarily egregious unless someone tells them so.

More and more federal agencies are agreeing to fund an outside evaluator, so consider using one (or plan for one in your next proposal). Evaluators are expensive, but they help both the grantor and grantee understand programs better and help others to replicate your successes.

If you encounter a problem in the project, go to the funder as quickly as possible and provide a full explanation. Don't let the funder find out through some other source that your program is not performing as planned. Most grantors will be very understanding and try to work with you if—and we emphasize *if*—you have been open, honest, and up-front with them from the beginning and behave that way about the problem.

Don't wait until the end of the year, or the end of the grant period, to say, "Sorry, we didn't meet our objectives." The funder must know what's happening early on and may be able to offer ideas for dealing with the difficulty. Or, at the very least, the agency or foundation will readjust its expectations for the project's outcome.

When there are unforeseeable costs, don't try to run your program on a serious deficit. Private sector grantors may be flexible enough to respond with additional funds—yet another reason why good relationships are important from the beginning. Some public agencies also may provide supplemental funds, though not as often. Even in the case of public agencies, the personal relationships are important. Many project officers intervene behind-the-scenes for the projects and people they favor.

Keep all data on how and why the problem developed. Even if you can't obtain supplemental funds during the current grant cycle, you'll need the information for future proposals.

Chapter 12

Being Kind to Funding Reviewers

I've reviewed proposals and I've spoken with reviewers and administrators at public agencies, private foundations, and corporations to find out what causes them to reject a proposal. Here's the "hit list" of mistakes to avoid:

- Ignoring directions given in the RFP.
- Failing to use the correct form.
- Using a typeface that is too small to read.
- Listing an incorrect "through" date for project length. The full period shown for the funds request must fall within the grantor's guidelines.
- Failing to include a Table of Contents, or including one with incorrect page numbers.
- Submitting a proposal with missing pages, pages that are out of place, or pages that are not numbered consecutively.
- Submitting a poorly edited proposal that contains spelling and grammatical errors.
- Spelling the name of your organization incorrectly. Yes! Some groups have done that! (In addition to hurting your image, this slows down processing and information retrieval.)
- Using acronyms or jargon specific to your organization's field.
- Stating, "We are the only ones who do this." (It's not only arrogant, it's probably wrong.)
- Striving to create an artificial connection with the grantor through the language or tone of the proposal.
- Failing to discuss potential obstacles or provide contingency plans.

- Submitting a budget that exceeds the maximum period allowed.
- Failing to provide appropriate breakdown and justification for each category of items in the budget.
- Failing to justify new equipment, or salary increases above the allowed annual adjustment, in subsequent grant years. Failing to provide source information for items receiving "other support."
- Providing inappropriate or irrelevant material in the Appendix.
- Submitting letters of support that don't clarify the relationship between supporters and the proposed program.
- Failing to include page numbers in the Appendix.
- Packaging Appendix sections together instead of fastening and labeling them separately.
- Neglecting to include duplicate originals of colored charts, graphs, or photographs for photocopying purposes.
- Binding the proposal so that pages cannot be removed for copying.
- Sending the proposal by FedEx or other overnight courier. Forgetting about manners. Being impolite, late and not acknowledging grantor's efforts or even saying "thanks."

Chapter 13

Select Samples

The following "Select Sample" attachments describe fictitious programs and grants. They are included to provide examples of how you can build grantseeking development and tracking tools. None of the foundations, individuals, organizations or projects cited is real.

Select Sample:
Private Funder Relationship
Management Chart

FOUNDATIONS		
SOURCE	**BACKGROUND**	**CONTACT LOG**
Apex Foundation 293 Flagler Hwy. E. Brookdale, FL 39104 **Telephone:** (728) 569-9050 **Contact:** Jon Parnell, Exec. Dir.; or Suresh Adami, Sr. Mgr., Contribs.	**Officers and Directors:** Roberta Q. Shuttlesworth, Pres.; Thomas Williams, V.P. and Exec. Dir.; Denise Cohen; Angel Martine, Esq.; Margaret T. Blankenhorn; Stephen Bates.	7/18: Cheryl to identify if appropriate target, and if so, who LOI should go to. 8/16: C. called M. Blankenhorn 9/19: C. met w/ Blankenhorn and Adami 10/02: Don and C. met with Adami and Parnell; will revisit early next year
Romulus Foundation 712 Fifth Ave. New York, NY 20086 **Telephone:** (212) 898-0211 **Contact:** Hilary Fong, Secy.	**Officers and Directors:** Arthur B. Sessions, Pres.; Hilary Fong, Secy.; Avery Totham, C.F.O.; Bernice Diamond; Leonard Foster; Vonna Schmidt.	7/18: Don and board to identify if any existing relationships can be used. 8/16: Board member Janet Stone will handle contact with A. Sessions 10/2: J. and D. in conference call with A.S., meeting to follow in Dec.

| The Citrus Fund 8672 Hwy. 11 Tampa, FL 31322 **Telephone:** (800) 766-4100 **Contact:** Darlene Martin, Grants Mgr. dmartin@citrusfund.org | **Mission:** To expand access to quality health care for underserved individuals and communities in Florida. **Program area(s):** The grantmaker has identified the following area(s) of interest: social health issues. | 7/18: Natasha and Don to identify if there are any relationships here; if not, LOI to be sent out ASAP 8/16: N. has phone conversation with D. Martin 9/17: D. and N. meet D. Martin |

CORPORATIONS		
SOURCE	**BACKGROUND**	**CONTACT LOG**
Margate Pharmaceuticals Alexis Stretton	Past Oakton funder	9/7: Don to contact A. Stretton re: interest 10/15: D. met with Stretton; LOI sent; response due by 12/1
Argon, Inc. Willis Parnel	N. has previous contact	7/1: N. calls Parnell re: interest 7/20: meeting scheduled, cancelled by Parnell 8/5: repeat contact attempts unanswered

Magee Laboratories Rosa Thal	Past funder and endorser of Oakton programs	7/6: D. to contact R. Thall 7/28: board member L. Saft has contact w/COO 9/10: D. and L.S. meet with Magee COO, Warren Pitts and R. Thall 10/19: LOI submitted
Veritas Manufacturing Dan Paulsen	Company has expressed an interest in program	8/6: N. contacts D. Paulsen 8/16: presentation to Paulsen 9/20: D. meets with D.P.

OTHER		
SOURCE	**BACKGROUND**	**CONTACT LOG**
FL Board of Corrections Raoul Nunez, Florence McGarvey	Funder of community-oriented programs related to prisons/jails	7/1: N. to find out steps to submitting unsolicited proposal and address to submit LOI 9/18: LOI sent
American Prison Operations	Have annual conference	9/16: D. to investigate benefits of associate membership
Correctional Organization of U.S.	Mainly prisons	7/5: N. contacts educational committee 7/28: discussion of future presentation possibilities
Prison Health Professionals Assn.		9/27: D. and N. attend seminar to build professional alliances

Select Sample: Letter of Intent (LOI)

Oakton Community Services
563 Mangrove Avenue
Gainesville, FL 31309

Date

Suresh Adami
Apex Foundation
293 Flagler Hwy. E.
Ft. Lauderdale, FL 39104

Dear Mr. Adami:

We at Oakton Community Services would like to partner with the Apex Foundation to develop a comprehensive training program for health and social service providers working with current or former prison inmates in Florida. Providers for the inmate community rarely have any training in prison life and culture, which can make them vulnerable and ultimately ineffective.

Our program would assist government, not-for-profit, and for-profit organizations to develop or improve upon inmate peer education and transitional case management services for currently incarcerated or recently released persons—many of whom have complex health and social needs.

OUR HISTORY AND MISSION:

For more than 25 years, Oakton has provided programs at various Florida county jails, state prisons, and federal correctional facilities. Current efforts include prevention case management services for prisoners with HIV/AIDS, literacy, family support, health education, parenting, policy, research, training and consultation and educational material development.

STATEMENT OF NEED:

Almost 2 million people are currently incarcerated in the United States, 25% of all people incarcerated worldwide. The overwhelming majority of these prisoners (>90%) will be released back into society, most of them within the next decade.

Most inmates are from lower socio-economic groups and (disproportionately) racial/ethnic minorities. They face daunting challenges to finding employment and re-integrating into society upon release. Over the past decade, an ever-growing inmate population has been returning to society with:

- The inability to identify and establish helpful relationships with health care and social service providers in the communities to which they are returning/being released;
- Fewer employable skills and/or coping skills for living in society;
- Older age and higher rates of common public health-concerns and chronic health problems such as STDs, hepatitis, etc.;
- High prevalence of drug and alcohol problems; and
- Higher rates of mental illness, including: Depression, Post Traumatic Stress Disorder, Anxiety Disorders, and various Axis II disorders, including: Fetal Alcohol Syndrome, Developmental Disorders, and Personality Disorders.

The proposed training program would provide government, not-for-profit, and for-profit organizations with the tools to effectively transition incarcerated persons back into the community upon release. Research shows that the recidivism rate of those leaving jail/prison with services is drastically lower than for those who receive no such transitional services.

TARGET AUDIENCES:

The proposed teaching modules would be developed for the following entities:

- Departments of Public Health that provide health and human services in urban areas with a high number of parolees;
- Community-based service organizations in urban areas with a high number of parolees; and
- Health Maintenance Organizations, Private Pay Organizations, pharmaceutical companies, and other companies providing services and products for ex-offenders.

Each training would be tailored according to the needs of the participating agencies and/or individuals.

GOALS AND OUTCOMES:

Our goal is to improve the knowledge and capacity of public health officials, social-service organizations, and pharmaceutical companies to work with incarcerated and newly released individuals. Anticipated outcomes include the ability to provide more culturally and socially appropriate services, resulting in better health and social outcomes for clients. Intermediate outcomes would be to improve the inmates' understanding of and ability to work with forensic health care providers, parole officers, and administrators. We intend to incorporate thorough evaluation techniques pre-and post-training.

PROGRAM DESCRIPTION:

This proposal presents a comprehensive training program including curriculum development, training implementation, and follow-up support. A series of 14 teaching modules is being developed by the clinical and administrative staff of Oakton to provide inmate peer education and transitional case management services. Please see attached for an outline of each specific module.

CONCLUSION:

A $250,000 grant for the proposed program would greatly increase Oakton's ability to improve services and opportunities for incarcerated persons being released back into the community, thus greatly decreasing the recidivism rate. We hope that this important program meets the Apex Foundation's philanthropic objectives and that we may jointly provide a solution to this problem.

Please contact me with any questions you may have about this proposed program.

Sincerely,

Donald Davis, Executive Director

Select Sample:
Community Relationship
Management Chart

CONTACT NAME	TITLE/ORG.	STAFF/BOARD LIAISON	ACTION LOG
Brenda Russel	Chair, Community Health Concerns	Natasha Dever (prog.dir.)	2/16: met to discuss proposed project; letter of support to follow by 3/31
Michael Jeon	Member, City Council	Don Davis (exec. dir.)	3/1: sent letter inviting a tour of existing site; met 3/19 re: service need in area
Paulette Ely	Vice President, Union Bank	Rafael Cruz (bd. member)	4/5: lunch meeting to identify business community's interest; John will present plan to Chamber on 6/1

Select Sample: Cover Letter

Caring United
5670 Lincoln Boulevard
Chicago, Illinois 63299-2100
(773) 989-0355

[date]

Paul Thornton
U.S. Department of Health and Human Services
200 Independence Avenue, S.W.
Washington, DC 20210

Dear Mr. Thornton:

Enclosed is our proposal for a program to create a network of faith-based HIV Testing and Wellness centers aimed at stopping the spread of HIV/AIDS among African-Americans by mobilizing Black Churches.

Thanks very much for giving thoughtful consideration to HHS funding for this proposal. We appreciate having the opportunity to make this submission.

If you or your staff have any questions, please call me anytime.

Very truly yours,

Jonelle Stevenson, Ph.D.
Founder and CEO

Select Sample:
Table of Contents

Caring United

Faith-Based HIV Testing and Wellness Project

Board of Directors

General Board of Religious Advisors

Certified Partnerships

Scientific and Community Advisory Members

Letters of Acknowledgement

African-American Clergy Declaration of War on HIV/AIDS

Copy of Organization 501(C)(3)

Most Recent Available Financial Audit

Organizational items of interest

Select Sample:
Proposal Summary

Caring United, a national organization whose mission is to stop the spread of HIV/AIDS among African-Americans by mobilizing Black Churches, is requesting funds to establish a network of faith-based HIV Testing and Wellness centers in 10 geographical locations throughout the United States. These networks of faith-based programs will be established in partnership with local public health providers and health departments.

Caring United is committed to combating the disproportionate prevalence of HIV/AIDS among African-Americans and thereby addressing other issues such as access to quality health care, care-seeking behaviors, and the well-being of African-American communities. Caring United's past achievements and future effectiveness are centered in ensuring that all people and communities most at-risk have access to early testing, treatment, and prevention programs.

The rate of HIV among African-Americans continues to increase at an alarming rate. One major factor is the persistence of denial, stigma, and the overwhelming failure of public health institutions to encourage individuals to get tested for HIV and, if positive, seek treatment and stop high-risk behaviors that transmit the virus.

The Black Church as an institution, as well as countless individual pastors, lay leaders, and congregation members have taken up the fight against HIV/AIDS and its devastating impact on Black America. As the single most important institution in the African-American community, the Black Church is strategically positioned to play a major role in the overall fight against HIV/AIDS and to encourage individuals to get tested for HIV.

Over the past twelve years, Caring United has built the capacity of thousands of Black church congregations to provide compassionate leadership in HIV prevention, treatment information, and supportive services to those infected and affected in their community. Caring United seeks to leverage the power and influence of the African-American church to:

- Position HIV testing as desirable and safe;
- Remove the stigma associated with HIV testing;
- Establish on-site HIV testing centers at churches (in selected cities);
- Provide supportive environments that encourage testing and support HIV-positive persons through the treatment process;
- Link HIV-positive people and affected people with treatment and support systems in their churches and communities; and
- Address health disparities within the African-American community.

Health education will provide the foundation of our testing and wellness programs. The programs will provide educational sessions, group counseling, individual counseling, and open discussions. The "wellness" component is designed to provide a safe space for African-Americans to examine the psychosocial issues and self-directed behaviors that perpetuate a cycle of high morbidity. The program will be designed to support individuals in making changes that would result in a healthy lifestyle.

Select Sample:
Introduction of Organization

Caring United is a 501(c)(3) organization based in Chicago whose mission is to stop the spread of HIV/AIDS among African-Americans by mobilizing and educating Black churches to become community centers for AIDS education and compassionate care. Caring United is a secular organization with a primarily faith-based constituency in multiple states. The organization's constituency is composed of churches and historically Black religious denominations as well as local, state, and national public health organizations, community-based organizations (CBOs), and AIDS service organizations (ASOs) in several states.

The programmatic goals of the organization are:

1. To build the capacity of Black church congregations to: provide compassionate leadership in the prevention of HIV; disseminate treatment information; and deliver supportive services to those infected and affected in their community.
2. To build the capacity of community-based organizations and state/local government agencies to collaborate effectively with Black churches to address the AIDS epidemic in the African-American community.
3. To raise awareness of the unique strength of the Black Church in facilitating the eradication of AIDS in the African-American community and of the need to support the church in this area.

Caring United's pioneering achievements have:

- Enabled thousands of churches to become leaders in preventing HIV by providing comprehensive educational programs and offering compassionate support to encourage those infected to seek and maintain treatment;
- Created strategies for educating and promoting communication among community-based organizations, state and local

government agencies, and Black churches to address the HIV/ AIDS epidemic; and

• Increased public awareness of the strengths of the Black Church as a unique resource in educating and mobilizing the African-American community to address AIDS.

The effectiveness of Caring United's programs is the result of on-going relationships with and endorsements from all major Black church denominations and caucuses as well as state and regional health agencies, individual churches, and community-based organizations. In addition, an aggressive outreach program engages Black church leaders, seminarians, and health professionals in the fight against HIV/ AIDS. Caring United combines a sound understanding of HIV/AIDS as a medical and social issue with profound and respectful insights into the needs and mission of the Black Church.

Educational and training programs include:

• Developing and disseminating culturally appropriate educational materials;

• Providing training, organizing, and technical assistance to individual churches, church groups, community-based organizations (CBOs), AIDS service organizations (ASOs), and public health departments on the national, state, and local level through a cooperative agreement with the Centers for Disease Control and Prevention;

• Assisting CBOs, ASOs, and health departments to deepen their understanding of the African-American community in order to engage the Black Church in increasing awareness of HIV/AIDS prevention and treatment through the annual Black Church Week of Prayer for the Healing of AIDS, the largest AIDS awareness program targeting Black America; and

• Providing mainstream national and local media as well as religious and African-American media with information about how the Black church meets the HIV/AIDS education needs of congregations and communities.

The organization is governed by a nine-member board of directors that is currently 100% African-American. In addition to staff and volunteers, the organization has a General Board of Religious Advisors consisting of executive-level leaders from 17 church denominations and two theological institutions. Denominations represented include: The National Black Catholic Caucus, Unity Fellowship, and the Church of God In Christ. The General Board meets once a year. Each member was selected by the denomination to participate.

Caring United works in partnership with the National Alliance of State and Territorial AIDS Directors (NASTAD) and National Minority AIDS Council (NMAC) to engage African-American clergy and congregants in community planning at the local level. and increase the capacity of the Black faith community to become an effective force in the fight against HIV/AIDS. This will help ensure that appropriate resources are channeled to their communities to fight HIV.

Table 1

African-American Church Denominations and Caucuses That Endorse Caring United

Denomination	Membership (Millions)	Year Founded
African Methodist Episcopal Church	3.5	1787
African Methodist Episcopal Zion	1.2	1796
Church	1.0	1870
Christian Methodist Episcopal Church	4.0	1897
Church of God In Christ	3.5	1881
National Baptist Convention of America	8.5	1895
National Baptist Convention, USA	1.2	1961
Progressive National Baptist Convention		

Black Caucuses within Mainstream Denominations
African-American Lutheran Association
Black Catholic Caucus
Black Methodists for Church Renewal
Black Presbyterians
Disciples of Christ National Convocation
Union of Black Episcopalians
United Black Christians

The organization has worked with most national African-American church leaders and is endorsed by every major national Black church denomination. Table 1 shows the wide support that Caring United has from Black church denominations and caucuses.

In addition, the organization has established a network of over 10,000 predominately Black churches nationwide to whom the organization has provided technical assistance or prevention education materials. Caring United has 56 established, certified network partners (health departments, community-based organizations, church-based coalitions, and civic organizations) that have been trained to educate, mobilize, and disseminate information to churches in their respective cities regarding AIDS education.

For many years, Caring United has had a special relationship with the University of Chicago School of Public Health (UCSPH). The organization will continue to avail itself of the assistance that can be provided by a strong partnership with an academic institution. Dr. Alexander Marshall, EdD, Associate Dean for Community and Minority Affairs at UCSPH, has served as Senior Evaluator for Caring United since 1995. Dr. Estelle Jackson, DrPH, Assistant Professor of Clinical Public Health at UCSPH, serves as Director of Project Evaluation and is a member of the Board of Directors.

Jonelle Stevenson, Ph.D., founder of Caring United and now its CEO, has been a pioneer in developing effective programs to educate and mobilize Black churches in the fight against AIDS.

Select Sample:
Problem Statement & Needs
Assessment

Despite the dramatic decrease in the national rate of AIDS-related deaths due to the availability and use of combination drug therapies, AIDS continues to devastate communities of African descent. These communities are confronting both increasing rates of HIV infection, as well as concomitant epidemics of other chronic diseases. According to the national Centers for Disease Control and Prevention (CDC):

- One in 50 African-American men and 1 in 160 African-American women are infected with HIV;
- Of the estimated 40,000 new HIV infections per year, more than half are in African-Americans (over 50 each day);
- Every day, seven Americans are newly infected with HIV, the virus that causes AIDS. Of the seven, three are African-American;
- AIDS is the leading cause of death for African-American women between the ages of 15 and 44;
- AIDS is one of the leading causes of death for all African-Americans between the ages of 25 and 44; and
- Of the 31,246 youth AIDS cases (13-24 years) reported through December 2000, 44% were African-American.

While the Minority HIV/AIDS Initiative targeting African-American and other minority communities resulted in an historically unprecedented $1.13 billion in new federal funding—$156 million in FY 1999, $245.4 million in FY 2000, $349 million in FY 2001, and $381 million in FY 2002—our nation is facing a steep decline in public and private budgets dedicated to HIV/AIDS and public health. A recent report from the Institute of Medicine (IOM) concludes that these disparities "contribute to higher death rates among minorities from cancer, heart disease, diabetes, and HIV infection."

The CDC reports that more than 200,000 Americans are living with HIV and do not know it. The alarming statistics regarding HIV/AIDS in the African-American community indicates a large percentage of individuals are HIV positive and perhaps unknowingly passing the virus to others.

Church-based AIDS programs are essential to combat this problem. The proposed Caring United project will yield 30 church-based HIV testing and wellness centers within 10 U.S. cities. The program will build upon the established foundation of many Black churches having already become places of HIV/AIDS information dissemination.

While HIV testing and information dissemination will be the Caring United program's primary focus, its faith-based wellness centers will also provide group and individual counseling and community forums regarding health-care-seeking behaviors, access to health care, treatment adherence and the well being and health of African-Americans. To be selected for the program, each city must demonstrate the commitment of its local health department and public health institutions to work closely with Caring United in support of these faith-based HIV testing and wellness centers.

Select Sample:
Project Objectives

The goal of the proposed Caring United project is to increase the capacity of the Black faith community to become an effective force in the fight against HIV/AIDS by establishing HIV testing and wellness centers in three designated churches within 10 geographical locations over a period of five years.

This project will accomplish that goal through four activities: increasing HIV testing in Black communities and support services for HIV positive individuals; building the capacity of Black churches to serve as leaders in promoting HIV testing and overall good health and wellness among African-Americans; helping Black churches to provide AIDS education, HIV and treatment counseling, nutrition counseling, and referrals to other AIDS service organizations and public health services; and establishing strong support systems between faith-based HIV testing and wellness programs, local health departments, and public health institutions.

Specific objectives of the proposed project include:

1. Establishing an Advisory Board comprised of individuals from the religious, service provision, public health, and business management communities, as well as individuals living with HIV/AIDS who have experience with faith-based and community health programs.
2. Conducting an in-depth, replicative, and effective evaluation of two existing, successful church-based HIV testing programs.
3. Developing a protocol for the development and implementation of church-based HIV testing and wellness centers.
4. Developing criteria for the selection of church-based HIV testing and wellness centers.

5. Developing a protocol for the participation of church, public health agencies, and community leaders in the development and implementation of church-based HIV testing and wellness centers
6. Developing and implementing a communication and marketing plan designed to decrease the stigmatization of HIV and to encourage community participation in HIV testing and wellness centers
7. Developing and implementing 30 church-based HIV testing and wellness centers in African-American communities over a period of five years.

Through this project, Caring United will help improve access to HIV information and testing in African-American communities. As a result, HIV-positive individuals and their families will find better support and the communitywide rate of new infection will be lowered.

Select Sample:
Methods & Design

The proposed faith-based HIV testing and wellness centers will be modeled after two successful models currently in operation. Caring United will evaluate these programs to create a blueprint for replication and garner information that will be useful to other organizations attempting to establish or improve similar programs. A comparative case study approach will be used to understand program development and implementation within real life contexts.

This study will frame the design, structure, and implementation of the program. Topic areas will include program goals, targeted population, staffing, funding sources, specific program activities, and links with health departments, public health institutions and other community-based service providers. Detailed process information will be collected to compare actual activities and individuals served with the original program plan and target population.

An Advisory Board will be established comprised of individuals from the religious, service provision, public health, and business management communities and individuals living with HIV/AIDS who have experience with faith-based and community health programs. Members will organize themselves into two task groups: the public health task group and the business/community task group. Other subcommittees may be formed on an as-needed basis. Advisory group members will provide leadership throughout the five-year project period. Activities will be carried out primarily by conference call and exchange of written materials.

The advisory group team will develop criteria for the selection of church-based HIV testing and wellness centers, which will include:

- Highest geographical incidence of HIV/AIDS among African-Americans.

- Significant geographical increase of incidence of HIV/AIDS among African-Americans within the past five years.
- Level of church or church coalition involvement in HIV/AIDS education interventions within the past five years.
- Capacity of the church or church coalition to reach and influence African-Americans regarding HIV testing and wellness in the community at large.
- Capacity of the church or church coalition to execute the functions of an HIV testing and wellness center, including legal and confidentiality issues.
- Capacity of the church or church coalition to develop and maintain partnerships with health departments, public health institutions, and AIDS service organizations.
- Ability of the church or church coalition to develop the capacity to fiscally maintain the program after project end.
- Readiness of the community-at-large to support faith-based HIV testing and wellness centers.

The structure of the HIV testing model used in each center will be decided by the community coalition, which will be established in each geographical location. Community coalitions will include representatives from the local health department, public health institutions, AIDS service organizations, and others.

To create a uniform national program and model, Caring United will provide an on-site development and management team that will work within selected cities during the start-up phase of implementation. The team will work closely with selected churches and/or church coalitions, health departments, and public health institutions to establish partnerships and a framework in which each faith-based center will operate. The team will spend an initial three weeks within each city to provide capacity building in areas that include:

1. Community mobilization
2. Developing partnerships with public health agencies and other key community agencies
3. Management and organizational development

4. Staffing and staff development
5. Administrative and legal requirements
6. Funding and fiscal management
7. Building/physical space requirements
8. Marketing
9. Setting up referral network systems
10. Setting up of health education/wellness program structures
11. Evaluation

Two cities will be selected for program implementation in year one and year four. In years two and three of the program, centers will be implemented in three cities. Program implementation in year one will be considered the pilot phase of the program.

At the beginning of each program year, a one-week intensive retreat will discuss program goals, objectives, and structures and the in-depth social and psychosocial elements of HIV and health disparities among African-Americans. Representatives from each participating entity within every program city will be required to attend. The retreat will also foster networking among participants. Every year, representatives from previously established programs will attend the intensive retreat as trainers and experts, creating a peer education structure for church-based HIV testing and wellness centers.

A strong marketing campaign will provide a call to action from Black church leaders and congregations to empower and encourage African-Americans to get tested for HIV. This campaign will anchor the foundation of the proposed proposal by positioning Black churches as institutions that care and support persons living with HIV. This mass media campaign will position HIV testing as desirable, safe, and the responsible thing to do. Through television, print, radio, and publicity, the campaign will deliver these messages:

- It is socially acceptable and theologically responsible to get tested for HIV;
- Call Caring United for information on where you can get tested; and

- Contact Caring United to help your church be a place of information and support.

Program elements of the marketing campaign will include:

a. Media Campaign—national television, radio, and print
b. Special events in 10 cities selected for this program
c. Distribution of HIV testing educational materials
d. Publicity

Select Sample: Evaluation

Caring United measures and evaluates all of its programs under the directorship of its evaluation consultant, Dr. Alexander Marshall, EdD, associate dean of the University of Chicago School of Public Health. The evaluation goal of this project is to provide useful information about HIV testing programs run by faith-based institutions to help other cities, health departments, government agencies, and organizations establish or improve similar programs. A major aim will be to conduct an evaluation of the effectiveness and impact of each city's faith-based HIV testing and wellness center. Caring United will develop a case study protocol to document the replicability, effectiveness, and cost of each individual faith-based project as well as the design, structure, and implementation of the full program.

Effectiveness evaluation will document outcomes of this project at the program and service system levels. Questions to be answered will include:

- What needs and service inadequacies were experienced by the target population within each city prior to the institution of the faith-based HIV testing and wellness program?
- Did the program meet those needs or help overcome these inadequacies?
- What was the impact on other faith-based HIV programs and the larger congregation?
- Did activities by these institutions have an impact on the service environment for African-Americans?

Feedback from clients served will be gathered throughout the project to determine the significance of the program to them and levels of satisfaction with program services.

Select Sample:
Budget

Personnel:

Seven new staff members will be hired. Each will devote 100% of work time to the Caring United Program:

- Project Director will be responsible for day-to-day activities of the overall national program S/he will provide direction and supervision to the project field manager and project site coordinator and will be responsible for the successful operations of each faith-based HIV testing and wellness center. He/she will supervise the Administrative Assistant and clerical support staff.
- Project Field Manager will be responsible for the on-site development and management of each faith-based HIV testing and wellness center. H/She will be responsible for securing a firm program infrastructure, including staffing and staff development; management and organization development; administrative, legal, and fiscal requirements; and establishing strong partnerships with health departments, public health institutions, AIDS service organizations, and other key agencies required for the successful implementation of each HIV testing and wellness center. The director of each faith-based program will report to the project field manager. S/he will hold a master's degree in public health administration or business administration.
- Project Site Coordinator will be responsible for all aspects of program development and implementation within each center. S/he will work closely with staff and community members of each center to identify and implement appropriate health education programs, counseling services, and referral network systems. S/he will act as a public health technical advisor to each center throughout the project. S/he will hold a master's degree in pubic health or health education.

- Evaluation/Research Assistant will be responsible for the ongoing operation of data collection and other research activities and implementing research protocols. S/he will report to the director of project evaluation. S/he will be responsible for conducting interviews, collecting data and implementing evaluation protocol of both model programs. A master's level degree with experience directing projects in urban settings is desired.
- Media Coordinator will be responsible for all press-related activities and the implementation of the national publicity campaign. S/he will be responsible for every aspect of production and media relations and will establish strong linkages with communications structures within the geographical location of each center. A master's degree with five years' experience in media relations is desired.
- Administrative Assistant will be responsible for the daily management of financial matters regarding the grant, ordering supplies and equipment, making travel arrangements and maintaining petty cash. S/he will oversee report preparation, coordinate mailings and other activities. An experienced office manager/administrator will be sought for this position.
- Clerical Support will provide assistance answering phones, typing, filing, keeping records, preparing mailings, and other tasks undertaken by the project team. This is an entry-level position.

Several current Caring United staff members will devote portions of their time to the project. They include:

- **Jonelle Stevenson, Ph.D.**, founder and CEO, who will provide overall direction and guidance for the development and implementation of the project and will direct the activities of the staff, advisory task group, and community mobilization efforts in each geographical location. She will help select each testing and wellness site, write reports and serve as national spokesperson. She will devote 40% of her time to the project.
- **Alexander Marshall, Ed.D.**, will serve as senior evaluator, chair of the Advisory Board, and an important link between

Caring United and a range of public health and community evaluation research expertise. Dr. Marshall will contribute 10% of his time to the project.

- **Estelle Jackson, Ph.D.**, will serve as director of the project evaluation. She will oversee development of the replicative evaluation and protocol development, prepare evaluation research designs for the overall program, and direct the evaluation/research assistant. She will conduct data analyses and prepare technical reports. Twenty percent (20%) of her time will be secured from the University of Chicago School of Public Health to be devoted to this project.

- **Brandon Lyle-Hawthorne, MBA**, will serve as director of communications and marketing. He will develop effective strategies to ensure that each faith-based HIV testing and wellness center, as well as the national program, is presented in culturally appropriate formats and venues to be most accessible and beneficial to Black faith leaders and their communities. He will devote 30% of his time to the project.

- **Cynthia Castle**, technical writer, will write all protocol documents for program development, management and daily operations, and legal requirements regarding HIV testing. She will translate all technical research reports and will write the brochure on HIV testing and periodic newsletters. She will devote 30% of her time to this project.

- **Martin Wooding**, MIS specialist, will develop the program's management information system and supporting programming, data entry, and data analysis activities in all testing and wellness centers. He will develop protocols for transfer of data and linking information from different data collection activities. He will devote 30% of his time to this project.

Total Personnel Cost: $200,000

Fringe Benefits: The current fringe benefit rate is 25 percent of personnel costs.

Travel: Estimated cost for four staff (CEO, project director, field manager, site coordinator) to conduct three visits in selected cities per year—including an initial three-week stay by project field manager and site coordinator—is estimated at $60,000 for year one and year four, and $90,000 for years two and three; $25,000 for a final visit in year five. Estimated cost for annual conference for all participants in each state, over five years, is $275,000. Estimated cost for annual advisory board meeting is $25,000 per year.

Equipment: Six computers, two laptops, and two printers will be purchased for staff to perform their duties effectively. In the field, staff will use laptops. Four large file cabinets will be purchased for records storage. Estimated cost: $30,000, first year only.

Supplies: General office supplies (paper, pens, toner, file folders, etc.) are estimated at $6,000 per year.

Other:

    a. Postage is estimated at $20,000 per year for mailings to churches, health departments, and other agencies; a national newsletter will be mailed to the entire Caring United database highlighting the program and encouraging faith-based organizations to encourage African Americans to get tested.

    b. Printing, design, and reproduction for all materials—including reports, evaluation tools and newsletters—is estimated at $37,500 per year.

    c. Telephone/fax/Internet cost is estimated at $15,000 for each year. This cost reflects usage for long distance and regional calls, voice mail, and e-mail.

    d. Each participating church will receive $25,000 per year for operational expenses upon their entry into the program. Estimated cost over five years is $2,625,000.

Indirect Cost: Indirect cost is estimated at 33% of the program cost per year, including office rent, utilities, insurances, equipment usage, etc. Estimated cost: year one, $409,695; year two, $483,945; year three, $558,195; year four, $597,795; year five, $586,245.

Important Budget Considerations from the Funder's Point of View

- Is your budget request in line with the type and size of other grants given by your funder?
- Does your budget include all requested items and follow formatting guidelines?
- Are your project budget requests in line with the organization's operating budget?
- Does your budget reflect the program you described in the narrative section of the proposal?
- Is your budget accurately justified by the projected outcomes of the project?
- Is there community support shown in your budget? < expenses? your all justify to able you>
- Have you double-checked to make sure your calculations are correct?

Online Funding Resources

Government Resources

Catalog of Federal Domestic Assistance

www.cfda.gov

Provides a database of all grants available within each federal agency. Grants are searchable in a variety of ways and are updated on an ongoing basis.

Centers for Disease Control and Prevention—Funding Opportunities

www.cdc.gov/funding.htm

Lists all CDC funding opportunities including links to CDC grant information and applications.

Federal Grant Opportunities

www.fedgrants.gov

Allows the grantseeker to cull government grants by agency, office, posting date, activity category, CFDA code and eligibility. Site also offers email notification for new grant announcements.

FedStats

www.fedstats.gov

Provides statistics from more than 100 US Federal Agencies and includes links to statistical agencies.

First Government

www.firstgov.gov

Official site that links to and navigates through all US Government websites.

Grants.gov

www.grants.gov

"The electronic storefront for Federal grants." Searches grants several ways and also offers email notification for new grant announcements.

GrantsNet

www.hhs.gov/grantsnet

Provides access to federal agency grants. The site offers the "Electronic Roadmap to Grants," which includes information on finding Department of Health and Human Services (DHHS) grants, and other DHHS funding resources.

National Institutes of Health Funding Opportunities

www.nih.gov/grants

Provides information about NIH grants and other funding opportunities as well as information about applying for those grants.

NonProfit Gateway

www.nonprofit.gov

A branch of the official site for the US government (FirstGov), specifically designed for not-for-profit organizations. Resources include such topics as fundraising, grants, loans, tax and legal information, as well as agency specific resources and other government links.

US Census Bureau

www.census.gov

Provides various kinds of data, including statistics on poverty and housing.

Non-Government/Private Resources

Council on Foundations

www.cof.org

Membership organization of more than 2,000 worldwide grantmaking foundations and giving programs. Site offers leadership expertise, information about legal services, networking opportunities and various other services.

The Foundation Center

www.fdncenter.org

Provides various grantseeking resources including more than 74,000 foundation profiles, educational information, and philanthropy-related statistics. Membership is required to gain access to certain informational tools on the site.

Grantsmanship Center

www.tgci.com

Offers information about grants, publications, and grantsmanship. TGCI makes available on CD-Rom each year the best federally-funded grant proposals.

GrantSmart

www.grantsmart.org

A resource center for and about the not-for-profit community with data about private foundation activities.

Kaiser Family Foundation—State Health Facts Online

www.statehealthfacts.kff.org

Provides state comparisons by health topic including the uninsured, AIDS and minority health, as well as individual state profiles.

Kaiser Network

www.kaisernetwork.org

Provides current information on health policy initiatives.

National Committee for Responsive Philanthropy

www.ncrp.org

A national watchdog, research and advocacy organization that promotes public accountability and accessibility among foundations, corporate grantmakers, individual donors and workplace giving programs. Site includes a detailed list of links to various philanthropy resources.

Public Health Foundation

www.phg.org

PHF is dedicated to supporting efforts of local, state and federal public health agencies and systems to achieve healthy communities through research, training and technical assistance. Site includes information about their current programs and initiatives.

Robert Wood Johnson Foundation

www.rwjf.org

RWJ funds a variety of projects to improve the health and health care of all Americans. Site includes detailed information about current grant opportunities as well as corresponding application forms.

United Way

www.unitedway.org

Site provides various resources as well as details about the grants, programs, and services offered by United Way around the country.

Glossary of Terms

A

Annual Report—A voluntary report issued by a foundation or corporate giving program which provides financial data and descriptions of grantmaking activities. Annual reports vary in format from simple typewritten documents listing the year's grants to detailed publications which provide substantial information about the grantmaking program.

Appropriated Funds—Money set aside by Congress to be spent in the following fiscal year for specified projects or programs.

Appropriations Committee—The actual committee designated in the House of Representatives and Senate with responsibility to give final approval to fund designated programs.

Assets—The amount of capital or principal—money, stocks, bonds, real estate, or other resources of the foundation or corporation.

Authorized Funds—Money which Congress initially allocates for needed projects or programs. Until this money is appropriated, it cannot be spent.

B

Budget—Itemized list of expenditures and income that is written as part of a proposal.

Budget Reconciliations—One of the last stages in the budget process whereby spending limits and funding requirements are matched within specific government agencies and departments.

Budget Resolution—First action taken by Congress on a new budget's legislative journey. This is an initial approval of spending limits and guidelines for a broad range of projects or programs.

C

Capital Support—Funds provided for endowment purposes, buildings, construction or equipment.

Challenge Grant—A grant award that will be paid only if the donee organization is able to raise additional funds from another source(s). Challenge grants are often used to stimulate giving from other donors. (See also Matching Grant.)

Community Foundation—A 501(c)(3) organization which makes grants for charitable purposes in a specific community or region. Funds are usually derived from many donors and held in an endowment independently administered; income earned by the endowment is then used to make grants. Although a few community foundations may be classified by the IRS as private foundations, most are classified as public charities eligible for maximum income tax-deductible contributions from the general public. (See also Public Charity.)

Company-Sponsored Foundation (also referred to as Corporate Foundation)—A private foundation whose grant funds are derived primarily from the contributions of a profit-making business organization. The company—sponsored foundation may maintain close ties with the donor company, but it is an independent organization with its own endowment and is subject to the same rules and regulations as other private foundations. (See also Private Foundation.)

Competitive Grant—Award for specific types of research, demonstration, training, etc.

Contract—An agreement between the government and an individual or organization to perform a specific work order, job or function for a specified amount of money. This work is designed and specified by the government, versus a grant, which is most often designed by the non-government party.

Cooperative Venture—A joint effort between or among two or more grantmakers (including foundations, corporations and government agencies). Partners may share in funding responsibilities or contribute information and technical resources.

Corporate Giving—Corporations may choose to give by means of a company foundation, a separate corporate giving program, or both. Company foundations file form 990PF. Researching corporate giving programs can be more difficult since their tax returns are not in the public record.

Corporate Giving Program—A grantmaking program established and administered within a profit-making company. Corporate giving programs do not have a separate endowment and their annual grant totals are generally or directly related to current profits. They are not subject to the same reporting requirements as private foundations. Some companies make charitable contributions through both a corporate giving program and a company-sponsored foundation.

D

Demonstration Grant—Funds used to underwrite a feasibility study or program (e.g., to test the assumption that a new drug rehabilitation program actually works).

Demonstration Project—A first-of-a-kind project funded by the government in hopes of demonstrating to others how to educate, deliver services or establish new research methodologies. Such projects, when proven successful, are often replicated by others.

Direct Costs—Cost items directly related to producing the end project or providing services specified in the grant or contract. Direct costs include labor, other direct costs, indirect costs, overhead costs and general and administrative costs.

Distribution Committee—The board responsible for making grant decisions for community foundations. It is intended to be broadly representative of the community served by the foundation.

E

Endowment—Funds intended to be kept permanently and invested to provide income for continued support of an organization.

Entitlement Grant—Noncompetitive and awarded automatically on basis of a legally-defined formula to all agencies or institutions that qualify (state, medical schools, etc.).

Expenditure Responsibility—In general, when a private foundation makes a grant to an organization which is not classified by the IRS as a public charity, the foundation is required by law to provide some assurance that the funds will be used for the intended charitable purposes. Special reports on such grants must be filed with the IRS. Most grantee organizations are public charities and many foundations do not make expenditure responsibility grants.

Extramural Funding—Monies used to finance projects or programs carried out by non-Federal government organizations or staff. This money is most often awarded in the form of grants or contracts.

F

Federated Giving Program—A joint fundraising effort usually administered by a nonprofit umbrella prganization which, in turn, distributes contributed funds to several nonprofit agencies. United Way and community chests or funds, United Jewish Appeal and other religious appeals, the United Negro College Fund and joint arts councils are examples of federated giving programs. (See also Community Fund.)

Fiscal Year (FY)—A 12-month accounting period, which for the federal government runs from October 1 of one calendar year to

September 30 of the next. Monies appropriated for any given fiscal year must be spent by the last day of that fiscal year.

Financial Statements—Schedules that detail all the financial activities of an organization usually prepared at the end of a fiscal year. These usually include a balance sheet and an income statement.

Form 990PF—The annual information return that all private foundations must submit to the IRS each year and which is also filed with appropriate State officials. The form requires information on the foundation's assets, income, operating expenses, contributions and grants, paid staff and salaries, program funding areas, grantmaking guidelines and restrictions and grant application procedures.

Formula Grants—Awarded by federal agencies on the basis of a set formula, such as so many dollars per population, per capita income or enrollment. Chief recipients are state governments.

G

General and Administrative Costs—Expenses incurred by contractor/ grantee in the management and administration of the organization as a whole (e.g., accounting staff, legal expenses, expenses related to proposal preparation).

General Purpose Foundation—An independent private foundation which awards grants in many different fields of interest. (See also Special Purpose Foundation.)

General Purpose Grant—A grant made to further the general purpose or work of an organization, rather than for a specific purpose or project. (See also Operating Support Grant.)

Grant—Award of money or direct assistance to perform activity or programs whose outcome is seen as less certain than that from a contract, with expected results described in general terms. Applications can be submitted without having been solicited (unsolicited proposal) or through a program announcement (Request for Application or

RFA). Most federal grants fall into categories such as entitlement, competitive, block, categorical, demonstration, formula, matching, project and research grants.

Grant-Financial Report—A report detailing how grant funds were used by an organization. Many corporations require this kind of report from grantees. A financial report generally includes a listing of all expenditures from grant funds as well as an overall organizational financial report covering revenue, expenses, assets and liabilities.

Grassroots Fundraising—Efforts to raise money from individuals or groups from the local community on a broad basis. Usually an organization does grassroots fundraising within its own constituency—people who live in the neighborhood served or clients of the agency's services. Grassroots fundraising activities include membership drives, raffles, bake sales, auctions, benefits, dances and a range of other activities.

Guidelines—Procedures grantseekers should follow when approaching individual grantmakers.

I

Independent Foundation—A grantmaking organization usually classified by the IRS as a private foundation. Independent foundations may also be known as family foundations, general purpose foundations, special purpose foundations or private non-operating foundations. (See also Private Foundation.)

In-Kind Contributions—A contribution of equipment, supplies, or other property as distinguished from a monetary grant. Some organizations may also donate space or staff time as an in-kind contribution. (See also In-Kind Support.)

In-Kind Support—A non-monetary contribution of equipment, supplies or other property as distinguished from a grant. Some organizations may also donate use of space or staff time.

Indirect Costs—Or overhead costs. Cost items not directly related to producing a product or providing a service specified in a contract or grant, but rather costs incurred in maintaining contractor/ grantee personnel and facilities. These costs include overhead and administrative costs that cover rent, administrative personnel, furniture and other items that the contract/ grant do not specifically cover.

Indirect Cost Recovery—A principle by which indirect costs are funded through recovering costs through an agreed-upon rate (often used in government grant accounting).

L

Labor—Cost of hourly rate of personnel assigned to a project multiplied by the number of hours worked.

Legislative Intent—When Congress appropriates money for specific programs or projects, it is done through an agreed-upon budget. Committees often report how they feel or intend the money should actually be spent. Committee report language is not legally binding, but is often followed closely by those receiving the funding.

Level of Effort—An expression of the estimated amount of time required to complete a project, based on labor hours.

M

Matching Grant—A grant which is made to match funds provided by another donor. (See also Challenge Grant.)

Matching Grants/Funds—Funds or in-kind contributions that must be provided by the grantee or a third party. The funding source usually specifies what percentage of the project's cost must be in matching funds.

O

Operating Foundation—A 501(c)(3) organization classified by the IRS as a private foundation whose primary purpose is to conduct research, social welfare, or other programs determined by its governing body or establishment charter. Some grants may be made, but the sum is generally small relative to the funds used for the foundation's own programs. Very few operating foundations are also company-sponsored. These foundations commonly operate museums, libraries or research institutes.

Operating Support Grant—A grant to cover the regular personnel, administrative, and other expenses for an existing program or project. (See also General Purpose Grant.)

Other Direct Costs—Cost of all items, except direct labor, directly related to producing the end project. Examples include reproduction, printing, travel, telephone and supplies.

Overhead Costs—Expenses incurred by contractor or grantee in maintaining staff and facilities (e.g., rent, supplies, equipment, employee fringe benefits).

P

Payout Requirement—The minimum amount that private foundations are required to expend for charitable purposes (includes grants and, within certain limits, the administrative cost of making grants). In general, a private foundation must meet or exceed an annual payout requirement of 5 percent of the average market value of the foundation's assets. Corporate giving programs do not have to meet a payout requirement.

Peer Review—Advisory panel of experts from outside the government who make recommendations on the relative merit of applications. Used by most units of the federal government to review research and project grants.

Private Foundation—A nongovernmental, nonprofit organization with funds (usually from a single source, such as an individual, family or corporation) and program managed by its own trustees or directors, which was established to maintain or aid social, educational, religious, cultural or other charitable activities serving the common welfare, primarily through the making of grants. "Private foundation" also means an organization that is tax-exempt under Code section 501(c)(3) and is classified by IRS as a private foundation as defined in the Code. The code definition usually, but not always, identifies a foundation with the characteristics first described. (See also Public Charity.)

Program Officer—A staff member of a foundation or corporation who may have expertise in particular areas of grantmaking.

Program/Project Officer—Individual designated by sponsoring agency to serve as the official responsible for the scientific, technical and programmatic aspects of the grant project. Works closely with the grants management officer in the administration of grants.

Program-Related Investment (PRI)—A loan or other investment (as distinguished from a grant) made by a foundation or corporate giving program to another organization (including a business enterprise) for a project related to the grantmaker's stated charitable purpose and interests. Program-related investments are often made from a revolving fund; the foundation or corporation generally expects to receive its money back with interest or some other form of return at less than current market rates, which becomes available for further program-related investments.

Project Budget—The financial plan for a project for a specified period of time, showing both income and expense items.

Project Period—The total time for which support of a project has been approved, including extensions of time.

Proposal—A written application, often with supporting documents, submitted to a foundation or corporation in requesting a grant.

Public Charity—In general, an organization which is tax-exempt under Code section 501(c)(3) and is classified by IRS as a public charity and not a private foundation.

Public charities generally derive their funding or support primarily from the general public in carrying out their social, educational, religious or other charitable activities serving the common welfare. Some public charities engage in grant-making activities, though most engage in direct service or other tax-exempt activities. Public charities are eligible for maximum income-tax-deductible contributions from the public and are not subject to the same rules and restrictions as private foundations. Some are also referred to as "public foundations" or "publicly supported organizations" and may use the term "foundation" in their names. (See also Private Foundation.)

Q

Qualifying Distributions—Expenditures of private foundations used to satisfy payout requirement. These can include grants, reasonable administrative expenses, set-asides, loans and program-related investments and amounts paid to acquire assets used directly in carrying out exempt purposes.

Query Letter—A brief letter outlining an organization's activities and its request for funding sent to a foundation or corporate giving program to determine whether it would be appropriate to submit a full grant proposal. Many grantmakers prefer to be contacted in this way before receiving a full proposal.

R

Revenue—Income earned by an organization by selling goods or services.

RFA (Request for Application)—An announcement from a funding source that will result in a grant award.

RFP (Request for Proposal)—When the government issues a new contract or grant program, it sends out RFPs to agencies that might be qualified to participate. The RFP lists project specifications and application procedures. A few foundations occasionally use RFPs in specific fields, but most prefer to consider proposals that are initiated by applicants.

S

Seed Money—A grant or contribution used to start a new project or organization. Seed grants may cover salaries and other operating expenses of a new project.

Set-Asides—Funds set aside by a foundation for a specific purpose or project which are counted as qualifying distributions toward the foundation's annual payout requirement. Amount for the project must be paid within five years of the first set-aside.

Site Visit—Visit by persons responsible to funding agency to obtain additional information before the award of a contract. Site visits can also be made after contract or grant award to determine effectiveness of program.

Special Purpose Foundation—A private foundation which focuses its grantmaking activities in one or a few special areas of interest. For example, a foundation may only award grants in the area of cancer research or child development. (See also General Purpose Foundation.)

Sponsorship—Affiliation with an existing nonprofit organization for the purpose of receiving grants. Grantseekers are advised to either apply for federally tax-exempt status or to affiliate with a nonprofit sponsor.

Support—Income from gifts and grants.

T

Tax-Exempt—Refers to organizations that do not have to pay federal or state corporate tax, state sales taxes or telephone excise taxes. Individuals who make donations to such organizations can deduct these contributions from their income taxes.

Technical Assistance—Operational or management assistance given to nonprofit organizations. It can include fundraising assistance, budgeting and financial planning, program planning, legal advice, marketing and other aids to management. Assistance may be offered directly by a foundation or corporate staff member or in the form of a grant to pay for the services of an outside consultant. (See also In-Kind Contributions.)

Trustees—Foundation board members or officials who help make decisions about how grant monies are spent. Depending upon whether or not the foundation has paid staff, they may take a more or less active role in running its affairs.

Grantseeking Checklist

Getting Started

- Embrace the 3 guiding principles key to grantseeking (Chapter 1).
- Develop a clear and concise vision statement that represents your organization's core values (Chapter 2).
- Develop well-researched program ideas that are consistent with your mission (Chapter 2).
- Explore information-rich resources such as The Foundation Center and Catalog of Federal Domestic Assistance (CFDA) (Chapter 3).
- Identify the type of funding, public or private, that is best suited for your proposal (Chapter 3)
- Select the funders that may be a match with your organization (Chapter 3).
- Send a LOI to introduce your organization to the funders you have selected (Chapter 3).
- Meet with key foundation personnel to understand their philanthropic objectives and how they may help with your program (Chapter 3).
- Identify those who support your mission and use them and their contacts to build your web of support (Chapter 4).
- Tap into your board of directors as source of contacts and possible supporters (Chapter 4).
- Prepare talking points to use when meeting with supporters (Chapter 4).
- Meet with those you have identified as current and/or potential supporters to explain and share your mission and program plans (Chapter 4).

- Keep regular communication to nurture connections with your supporters. Remember to ask for written letters of endorsement (that you have drafted) (Chapter 4).
- Seek out and compile other forms of endorsement such as newspaper articles or community awards (Chapter 4).
- Evaluate your organization to know where you stand and what you need to improve (Chapter 5).

Ready to Apply

- Make a calendar of critical deadlines (Chapter 5).
- Read and reread RFP (3 times!) (Chapter 6).
- Highlight funding requirements and create a checklist (Chapter 6).
- Review grantwriting tools and tips (Chapter 7).
- Review the "hit list" of proposal mistakes to avoid (Chapter 12).
- Write your proposal (Chapter 7).
- Edit your proposal thoroughly, being sure to use a set of "fresh eyes" (Chapter 8).
- Check and double check that you have not missed any components of the proposal package, including supporting documents (Chapter 9).
- Make sure your proposal is packaged according to the directions and is addressed correctly (Chapter 9).
- Mail out your proposal, not at the last minute, but no more than 4 days in advance, preferably through regular or priority mail (using a private carrier such as FedEx is discouraged) (Chapter 9).

After You Apply

- Follow up with no more than one phone call about four weeks after proposal submission (do not follow up for public grants) (Chapter 10).
- Be prepared if the deciding board requires a visit to your site (Chapter 10).

- If you win—immediately send out thank-you letters and continue to provide your funder with updates (Chapter 10).
- Should you lose—immediately send out a thank-you letter and find out why you did not receive the grant, in order to improve future proposals (Chapter 10).
- After grants are announced, maintain your momentum and continue to be active in seeking out future funding and nurturing your relationships (Chapter 11).